A BITTER
WINTER

A BITTER WINTER

The Irish Civil War
1922–23

Colum Kenny

EASTWOOD BOOKS

First published 2022 by Eastwood Books
Dublin, Ireland
www.eastwoodbooks.com
www.wordwellbooks.com

1

Eastwood Books is an imprint of the Wordwell Group.

The Wordwell Group is a member of Publishing Ireland, the Irish Publishers'
Association.

Eastwood Books
The Wordwell Group
Unit 9, 78 Furze Road
Sandyford
Dublin, Ireland

ISBN: 978-1-913934-37-8 (Trade Paperback)
ISBN: 978-1-913934-38-5 (Epub)

British Library Cataloguing in Publication Data.
A catalogue record for this book is available from the National Library of
Ireland and the British Library.

Front cover image: John Lavery, 'Michael Collins (Love of Ireland)'. On 24 August
1922, Lavery painted the remains of his dead friend Collins in the chapel of St
Vincent's Hospital, Dublin, before they were taken by carriage to lie in state at City
Hall. At the last minute, Lavery added the inscription 'Love of Ireland'. That evening,
the Press Association reported that Lavery 'throughout today stood beside the coffin,
with a canvas before him […] The body has been embalmed and lies in a uniform
splashed with blood from the wound […] He lies dressed as he met his death, with
the ammunition pouch attached to his Sam Browne belt.' The painting was exhibited
at the Salon d'Automne, Paris, in November 1922. Courtesy Hugh Lane/Dublin City
Gallery

Typesetting and design by the Wordwell Group
Copyediting by Myles McCionnaith
Printed in Ireland by Sprint Print, Dublin

Cogadh carad, caoi námhad
(A war of friends is their enemy's opportunity)

– old Irish saying

CONTENTS

PREFACE

Writing about the Civil War, in a special centenary supplement published with the *Irish Times* on 9 May 2022, the Republic of Ireland's Minister for Culture, Catherine Martin TD, stated that official initiatives to remember that war would 'invite everyone to consider the painful legacies of our past and reach their own conclusions'. She promised, 'the State will not seek to communicate a preferred narrative or make judgments about any persons or actions.'

Martin's statement was well-intended, but troubling too. For she wrote as the representative of a democratic state that the defeated side in the Civil War had tried to smother at birth.

Meaningful remembrance of the Irish Civil War is not best done on the basis of a kind of moral equivalence, where sleeping dogs are let lie for fear of causing upset. For Irish public life continues to be dominated by parties largely grounded on factions of Sinn Féin in 1922–3. Two of those parties, Fianna Fáil and Fine Gael, now share power in a coalition government with Catherine Martin's Green Party, and are being closely challenged by a third, today's Sinn Féin. If people 'reach their own conclusions' about the Civil War, their conclusions are not necessarily equally valid. Politicians on their way to a duly elected Dáil Éireann were not legitimate targets in 1922, and nobody is entitled to hold or promote that view today without being robustly challenged. Suspension of judgment is unfair to the victims in 1922–3, and dangerous in 2022–3. Equivocation itself is 'a preferred narrative'. Either the effort to overthrow the emerging new state was fair game, or it was not, or it no longer matters. The distinguished historian F.S.L. Lyons, in 1971, felt that 'charity and the interests of truth alike demand a certain reticence about events which are still felt so profoundly' (*Ireland Since the Famine*, p. 460), but what does it mean that more than fifty years after he wrote we are still reluctant to make bold judgments? It signifies that questions of legitimacy and democracy that underpinned the Civil War have not entirely faded with the passing of the generations. Developments in the United States demonstrate how an even more remote civil war there (1861 to 1865) still reverberates through affairs of state today.

Sincerity alone is no protection against error or dangerous delusion. Instead of accepting realistically that they lacked popular support and sufficient resources to win whatever battle they thought they could win, the anti-Treaty republicans of 1922 might have devoted their energies to making the Free State economically and politically strong. They could have supported the democratically elected leaders Griffith and Collins – who believed that the Boundary Commission they had won by negotiation in London would mitigate the effect of the United Kingdom's partition of Ireland in 1920. All republicans might have thrown themselves constructively into ensuring from the outset that social policy was not determined by some of the most conservative forces on the island. Their war set back Ireland, especially by slowing the state's growth and poisoning public life for generations, and by giving Northern Ireland's government the time to stabilise its polity. As both sides fought, Irish nationalists could more readily be caricatured as inherently disposed to violent factionalism and feuding.

When one speaks casually of 'sides', it is of course a crude distinction. For each 'side' was a spectrum that included conservative and reformist tendencies. There were some pro-Treaty supporters who would have been happy to settle for a fairly limited form of Home Rule, while other pro-Treaty supporters such as Collins and Griffith saw the Treaty not as an end in itself but as a stepping-stone – as the freedom to achieve greater freedom. Some anti-Treaty fighters wanted a thirty-two-county socialist republic, while anti-Treaty politicians such as Éamon de Valera were considerably less radical.

The very epithet 'republican' is itself problematic. For many Irish people, it indicates little more than a wish to dispense with monarchy and its symbols. Irish 'republicans' make up a broad church of constitutional nationalists and revolutionary socialists. The word in Ireland is as much a rallying cry as a philosophy. In 1922, there was nothing about its use generally that suggested imminent laicisation (*laïcité*) of the type witnessed after 1870 in the French Third Republic. Indeed, the ideology and language of some of the most committed Irish republicans, such as that of the socialist Liam Mellows, was deeply Catholic in tone and content. The anti-Treaty occupation of the Four Courts was undertaken to coincide with the celebration of Christ's resurrection at Easter, just as the republican rising of 1916 had been.

Both 'sides' might have worked together, former comrades or friends reconciled to create, in peace, a practical constitutional framework for co-operation with unionists across the recently imposed border with Northern Ireland. In that territory, too, as may be too easily forgotten, a kind of secondary and sectarian civil war was brewing. With nationalists so divided, militant unionists in Ulster and right-wing Tories in London had their hands strengthened. The old Irish saying '*cogadh carad, caoi námhad*' (a war of friends is their enemy's opportunity) was never truer. Unfortunately, another Irish proverb has proven to be less accurate: '*ní buan cogadh na gcarad*' (a quarrel between friends/relatives is soon healed). The Civil War itself was short, but it has long borne bitter fruit.

Bill Kissane, in 2005, in his *Politics of the Irish Civil War* (p. 203), remarked that 'the dominant view' among historians was that the anti-Treaty side in the Civil War 'was very much in the wrong'. Yet it should also be said that if the Irish electorate had had a clear democratic choice between partition and an all-Ireland republic of some kind – a choice free from British and unionist threats of violence – then most voters on the island would almost certainly have opted for an all-Ireland republic and Sinn Féin would not have split. Rejection of the will of the majority on the island and continuing imperialism were at the root of the conflict. The island of Ireland had long been a political unit before 1920, albeit one with a large unionist minority, and small nations elsewhere in Europe were winning democratic sovereignty in the aftermath of the First World War. The pro-Treaty side did not run an Irish tricolour flag up the mast because the Irish Free State represented its ultimate ambitions, but because that form of state was seen as the best possible option in the face of repeated British threats of overwhelming force.

On 15 June 2022, at a conference about the Civil War at University College Cork, Taoiseach Micheál Martin said, 'There is every reason to believe that the war itself could have been avoided, and I believe that the tragedy of the first six months of 1922 was that the key figures in Dublin were never allowed a free hand to find a shared route forward. Constant interference and inflexibility from London was central to the fact that nothing came of these efforts.' Nonetheless, there had been 'constant interference and inflexibility from London' for centuries. Blaming the British is simply to restate the problem; it does not excuse a refusal by some republicans to accept the reality that the Irish public approved the Treaty as a pragmatic way forward – within which reality, the challenge was to engage in constructive democratic politics rather than destructive civil war. When Éamon de Valera wrote in 1937 in his preface to Dorothy Macardale's *The Irish Republic* that the antagonism of opposing principles and policies that ensued from the Treaty agreement 'was found incapable of reconciliation or peaceful adjustment', he merely stated the obvious. That the antagonism was 'found incapable' did not mean that it was necessarily incapable of reconciliation.

The peace agreement that Irish plenipotentiaries signed in London for Dáil Éireann in December 1921 was broadly welcomed throughout the twenty-six counties of the future Irish state, including by employer, farming and labour interests, by the Catholic church and even, in January 1922, by a majority of Sinn Féin members of the Dáil. But the emerging Irish government was soon embroiled in civil war. By the time it ended, in May 1923, the new state was battered and weakened – 'a pear-tree broken by the storm' in the words of W.B. Yeats. Verses quoted below at the start of each of the five seasons of civil war into which this book is divided are from that poet's 'Meditations in Time of Civil War'.

One of my great-grandfathers, Michael C. Kenny, was a member of the Fenians. Described at his death as 'a well-known '67 man', he had been 'out' in a brief revolt by its members in 1867. His son Kevin, my grandfather, produced for Patrick Pearse *An Macaomh* – the biannual journal of Pearse's St Enda's School

– and was responsible for managing the business side of some editions of Arthur Griffith's *Sinn Féin Year Book*. Kevin's son Michael, my father, tended to vote Fine Gael, while my mother Eileen Morgan admired Éamon de Valera (although not Charles Haughey). In writing this book, I have tried to be fair to all sides, not least out of consideration for my late parents' respective electoral sympathies.

The author wishes to thank for their assistance the National Library of Ireland, the Royal Irish Academy, Bray Public Library, the Churchill Archives Centre in Cambridge, Dublin City University, the Society of King's Inns, the National Archives of Ireland, the UK National Archives, UCD Archives, the University of Birmingham, Trinity College Dublin and the archivist of the Irish Defence Forces.

Ronan Colgan, Fiona Murphy and the team at Eastwood Books have been encouraging and enthusiastic in bringing to fruition the plan to publish a pair of accessible accounts of vital periods in the history of modern Ireland – last year, my *Midnight in London*, about the Anglo-Irish Treaty crisis of 1921, and now *A Bitter Winter*, about the Civil War.

My wife Catherine Curran has been very supportive, as usual. This book about war is dedicated in the year of their birth to our two granddaughters, Aoife and Sophie, in the hope that their generation will enjoy many years of peace and well-being in a just and democratic world.

SPRING 1922

We had fed the heart on fantasies,
The heart's grown brutal from the fare;
More substance in our enmities
Than in our love;

Standing by the Treaty

'What I have signed I shall stand by in the hope that the end of the conflict of centuries is at hand,' wrote Arthur Griffith, founder of Sinn Féin. Was it anxiety stirred him to cross out 'hope' and replace it with the firmer word 'belief', before issuing his message to the world press? All five members of the team he led to London – including Michael Collins –had just signed a peace deal with the UK government. One month later, on 7 January 1922, a majority of Sinn Féin MPs approved that deal for a treaty. But others soon opposed it by force.

Griffith and Collins could not have won a fully independent all-Ireland state at a table in London – not when the republican Volunteers had failed to win one by their War of Independence. From 1919 to 1921, a war of liberation from Britain had been waged across Ireland, alarming people and curtailing economic life. During it, the United Kingdom Government of Ireland Act 1920 partitioned Ireland. On 7 June 1921, Northern Ireland's new parliament met for the first time. A Northern Ireland government was established under the unionist James Craig. Contrary to a widespread misconception, Ireland was actually partitioned *before* Treaty negotiations began.

On 9 July 1921, a truce was declared in the War of Independence. As president of Dáil Éireann, Éamon de Valera immediately went to England, where four times that month he and Prime Minister Lloyd George met alone. Only in October did formal negotiations begin. Their agreed purpose was 'to ascertain how the association of Ireland with the community of nations known as the British Empire can best be reconciled with Irish national aspirations'. Remarkably, de Valera himself did not lead the Irish in October. Instead, he asked Griffith to chair a team of five plenipotentiaries. Lloyd George led the British side.

On 7 October 1921, de Valera wrote to the plenipotentiaries, outlining what he 'understood' would be their mode of proceeding. His letter was headlined 'instructions', but in it he conceded that they had 'full powers' to negotiate and conclude a treaty, as defined in their credentials from Dáil Éireann. The plenipotentiaries were to ask him a number of times to join them in London, but for reasons he explained differently at various times, he remained in Ireland. Nevertheless, the delegates in London kept de Valera closely informed and on 6 December 1921 finally signed an agreement with the British – one that was not binding unless and until approved by the Irish Cabinet and by a majority of members of parliament elected in that part of Ireland about to become an independent state.

During negotiations in London, the pre-existing partition of Ireland was addressed, with Griffith and Collins seeking to modify it. Their team agreed to a boundary commission that was included in the final Treaty. They expected this commission to make decisions based on the wishes of people locally in Ulster. Given recent voting patterns, they were confident that this would result in Tyrone, Fermanagh and some other areas of Northern Ireland passing into the territory of the Irish Free State. However, civil war erupted in 1922, and both Griffith and

Collins were soon dead. The border would stay as it was when defined by Britain in 1920. The present author has cautioned in *Midnight in London: The Anglo-Irish Treaty Crisis 1921* (2021) and in *History Ireland* (July/August 2022) against relying uncritically on Frank Pakenham's influential 1935 book *Peace by Ordeal* for an account of the Treaty negotiations.

The plenipotentiaries also negotiated the withdrawal of British armed forces from the twenty-six counties of the Irish Free State, although the British Navy was to continue to have use of particular Irish ports in defined circumstances. The Irish delegates also ensured that a proposed oath to be taken by members of Dáil Éireann would be changed, so that it involved swearing an oath of faithfulness rather than an oath of allegiance to the British monarch. Even as altered, this oath and the symbolical position of the King were bitter pills to swallow for all members of Sinn Féin and for many other Irish people.

The delegates returned to Ireland in early December, amid angry assertions that they had exceeded their powers by not seeking full Irish Cabinet approval of the very final draft agreement *before* signing it. Instead, they had put their names to the agreement subject to Irish Cabinet and Dáil Éireann approval *after* signing it. They did so because they feared that Lloyd George's ultimatum – that they must sign the proposed agreement as it stood on 6 December or face an immediate end to the talks and a renewal of British hostilities – was no bluff. If it were not a bluff, the British Army this time would be recovered from war in Europe and would no longer have to rely on ragged forces of Black and Tans or Auxiliaries to fight in Ireland.

By four votes to three, the Cabinet in fact approved the agreement. De Valera was in a minority, with Cathal Brugha and Austin Stack, because W.T. Cosgrave sided with the three ministers who were part of the negotiating team in London, namely Griffith, Collins and Robert Barton.

There followed over Christmas a long and acrimonious debate in Dáil Éireann. When a vote was finally taken, on 7 January 1922, the proposed Treaty was approved by 64 votes to 57. De Valera stepped down as president of Dáil Éireann and Griffith replaced him. The Dáil was more militant on the issues involved than was the country at large – as would become more apparent following the general election of June 1922, when the proportion of anti-Treaty deputies was reduced considerably.

Matters were about to pass out of the democratic sphere and into a military arena. During 1922, the defeated minority sought to assert itself by other means, leading to civil war. Some were convinced that the British were bluffing. Some believed that Irish Republican Army volunteers could defeat the British Army in an outright war, perhaps overcoming Ulster Unionist opponents in the process to declare an all-Ireland republic. Some simply hoped to force a better compromise, perhaps by the removal of any oath to the monarch, along with the freedom to style the new twenty-six-county state a republic and to elect a president instead of accepting the monarch or a governor-general as head of state. Nevertheless, senior military figures on the pro-Treaty side knew intimately the current state of the IRA and its armaments, and were far from confident that they could even sustain a short struggle of the kind fought up until the truce of July 1921. They were conscious of the strength of the armed loyalist Ulster Volunteers and of a British Army freed from war in Europe. They were also aware that Irish people were weary of war. They wished to try peace for a while.

DEMOCRACY AND SINN FÉIN

etween December 1918 and June 1922, three general
elections reflected a sea change in Irish politics. In 1918,
a united Sinn Féin surged to victory for the first time and
immediately founded the 1st Dáil; then, in 1921, all its candidates were returned unopposed and convened the 2nd Dáil; in
June 1922, Sinn Féin's pro-Treaty candidates performed better
than its anti-Treaty candidates.

The Irish Labour Party stepped aside from the contests in
1918 and 1921 in order to give voters a straight choice on the
question of independence. In 1922, however, Labour and other
non-Sinn Féin candidates ran against pro-Treaty and anti-Treaty
Sinn Féin candidates. The anti-Treaty Sinn Féin candidates were
the only ones opposing the Treaty, and they filled barely a quarter of the seats in the 3rd Dáil.

FIRST ELECTION – 14 DECEMBER 1918

All Ireland voted in a UK general election, for 105 Irish seats
at Westminster (1st Dáil created).

Before the 1916 Easter Rebellion, Sinn Féin had been an insignificant electoral force at national level. In 1918, invoking the martyrs of the 1916 Rising and having opposed military conscription, it won 73 of the 105 Irish seats at Westminster (25 without a contest). It trounced the old Irish Parliamentary Party that had failed to deliver Home Rule for Ireland. The IPP took just six seats.

Unionists won twenty-two seats, with three candidates from a Labour Unionist grouping and one Independent Unionist from Dublin University (i.e. Trinity College) also being elected.

This was the last occasion on which all Ireland voted in a UK general election. It did so on the basis of a greatly extended electoral roll that included some women for the first time. Sinn Féin MPs did not take their seats in London but instead established, in January 1919, the revolutionary 1st Dáil Éireann in Dublin.

SECOND ELECTION – 24 MAY 1921

The twenty-six counties of the future Irish Free State returned representatives for 128 seats (2nd Dáil).

All 124 Sinn Féin candidates were returned unopposed, including from the National University of Ireland. Dublin University returned four Independent Unionist candidates, also unopposed.

The British had called this election under the UK Government of Ireland Act 1920, which partitioned Ireland. Section 1 of the act established 'Parliaments of Southern and Northern Ireland'. Sinn Féin candidates in 'Southern Ireland', when returned, sat as the 2nd Dáil.

THIRD ELECTION – 16 JUNE 1922

The twenty-six counties, or nascent Irish Free State, voted for 128 seats (3rd Dáil).

This was the Pact election (discussed later), which pro-Treaty and anti-Treaty members of Sinn Féin agreed to hold and which revealed clearly that the public at large was not as closely divided on the Treaty question as the Dáil itself had been when it voted in January 1922 to accept the agreement for a Treaty. The anti-Treaty candidates now won only a little more than one quarter of the seats available. Thus, while anti-Treaty Sinn Féin took 36 seats (of which sixteen were unopposed), pro-Treaty Sinn Féin took 58 (seventeen unopposed). Labour, the Farmers' Party and independents won seventeen, seven and ten seats respectively. As regards the first choice ('first preference') of voters in the constituencies that were contested, just 21.8 per cent or under a quarter chose anti-Treaty Sinn Féin candidates, 38.5 per cent pro-Treaty Sinn Féin candidates and a notable 39.6 per cent opted for candidates contesting from other parties or individual independents.

LIMERICK PROVOCATION

On 9 February 1922, the British Army revealed its plans for evacuating Limerick under the Treaty. Liam Forde, commander of the mid-Limerick IRA, publicly rejected the Treaty and seemed set to occupy all strategic military facilities in Limerick formerly in British hands. As anti-Treaty and pro-Treaty forces strengthened their respective positions there, Captain Bill Stapleton of the National Army – formerly a very active member of Michael Collins's assassination squad (BMH WS 822) – was shot and wounded by anti-Treatyites. Stapleton was in charge of John Street Barrack. He was entering a hotel in the city, unaccompanied, on the night of Thursday, 2 March when he was 'followed by five civilians into the coffee room where the order "Hands up" was given'. He turned around, 'whereupon a revolver shot was fired point blank at him, the bullet passing through the muscle of the left arm. He staggered and was overpowered by two of the civilians who relieved him of his revolver and disappeared' (*Cork Examiner*, 4 March). If this was the first shot of the Civil War, it did not lead to immediate widespread hostilities. But tensions were rising.

Ernest Blythe was then Dáil Éireann's Minister for Trade. He later recalled that 'as early as February 1922, when a clash occurred over the proposed occupation of the Limerick barracks by General Michael Brennan's forces, a joint meeting of members of the Provisional Government and Dáil Éireann Cabinet held in the drawing-room of the Mansion House, practically decided to fight immediately. Griffith, as never before at such a meeting, stood up and made a formal speech. He called for military action to maintain order and assert the authority of the Government and people. Collins was in an angry mood because of treatment he had received in Cork and assented to Griffith's proposal.' Blythe wrote that other ministers, 'alarmed by the increasing signs of a drift towards anarchy', were willing to agree. But then General Richard Mulcahy urged that the pro-Treaty forces were not yet ready, 'from the point of view either of psychology or even of military training', to carry out satisfactorily the suggested operation in Limerick. Blythe added, 'Collins was instantly convinced by what General Mulcahy said. Thereafter, the difficulty was to bring Collins up once again to the point of actually giving the order to fight' (*Irish Times*, 27 Nov. 1968).

Throughout Ireland in early 1922, there was a standoff, with many former comrades from the IRA slow to clash fatally with old friends. Each side occupied barracks and other buildings in various towns. There was a fierce two-day gun-fight in Kilkenny city in early May, after anti-Treaty forces took over Kilkenny Castle and the tower of St Canice's Cathedral among other positions. The National Army drove them out; there were injuries but no reported deaths. Meanwhile, the government was building up a national army with new recruits as it prepared to exert its full authority.

De Valera's Warnings

In March 1922, the *Cork Examiner* reported that Éamon de Valera had just given a speech to a crowd of about two thousand people in Carrick-on-Suir, Co. Tipperary. Accompanied by armed IRA members, he warned, 'If Ireland accepts the Treaty then full freedom can be got only by civil war in Ireland.' He added, 'If the Treaty is accepted the fight for freedom will still go on, and the Irish people, instead of fighting foreign soldiers, will have to fight the Irish soldiers of an Irish Government, set up by Irishmen. If the Treaty is not rejected perhaps it is over the bodies of the boys and young men he saw around him that day the fight for Irish freedom may be fought.'

On 17 March, the *Irish Times* quoted de Valera saying, 'If you don't fight to-day you will have to fight to-morrow, and I say, when you are in a good fighting position, then fight on.' The *Irish Independent* reported that at Dungarvan he proclaimed, 'It was only by civil war after this they could get their independence.' At Thurles (as the *Irish Independent* of 18 March, and other papers later, reported) he said that if the Treaty was accepted, then the Volunteers of the future would 'have to wade through Irish blood, through the blood of soldiers of the Irish Government, and through, perhaps, the blood of some of the members of the Government in order to get Irish freedom'.

Yet he had struck a different note the previous year when, as president of the Dáil, he was trying to set up Treaty talks with the British. In the Dáil on 23 August 1921, just weeks after a truce in the War of Independence was declared, he forecast disagreements, 'It is obvious that whenever there are negotiations, unless you are able to dictate terms you will have differences. Therefore it is obvious you will have sharp differences. The policy of the Ministry [his Cabinet] will be that which they consider would be best for the country. The Ministry itself may not be able to agree and in such a case the majority would rule.' He added a line that indicated he did not contemplate himself being in a minority. This was, 'Those who would disagree with me would resign.' He also said then that

> If the plenipotentiaries go to negotiate a treaty or a peace, seeing that we are not in the position that we can dictate the terms, we will, therefore, have proposals brought back which cannot satisfy everybody, and will not; and my position is that when such a time comes I will be in a position, having discussed the matter with the Cabinet, to come forward with such proposals as we think wise and right. It will be then for you either to accept the recommendations of the Ministry or reject them.

From further newspaper reports, it appears that on 19 March 1922, de Valera in Killarney warned, 'Those who wanted to get on and travel on the road to achieve freedom, such as those men present with their rifles, would have in the future not merely the foreign soldiers to meet, but they would have to meet the forces of their own brothers, their fellow-countrymen, who would be supporting the government' (*Irish Independent, Nationalist* and

Freeman's Journal, 20 March). According to the *Cork Examiner* of 20 March, he also said at Killarney that weekend that 'The people had never a right to do wrong. He was certain that the same pluck which had carried them so far would enable them to finish (cheers).'

On 21 March 1922, the political correspondent of the *Irish Times* wrote that 'Mr. de Valera's wild speeches, with their threats of civil war, have been read everywhere with amazement, in view of his earlier declarations – especially that in Paris during the Race Congress, in which he declared that there would be no internal dissensions, and that the will of the people must prevail.' De Valera distinguished between warnings and threats and, in Dáil Éireann on 19 May 1922, he said, 'I denied in the *Irish Independent* that I made this statement [about wading through Irish blood, including that of government ministers], and the thousands of people who listened to me know it is a lie.' Séamus Robinson, an anti-Treaty deputy and IRA commander in Tipperary, told the Dáil that he had been present and he backed de Valera's version. However, in his letter to the *Irish Independent* published by that paper on 23 April 1922, de Valera had actually quoted and appeared to confirm that he made at Thurles statements about wading through the blood of Irish soldiers and government ministers, while claiming 'This a child might understand, but you [editor] depart from its plain meaning in order to give the infamous lead in misrepresentation.' He did not deny saying the words.

Historians have commented on de Valera's proclivity to give incompatible explanations of his actions at different times, with John Bowman in one essay observing that de Valera 'never lost his genius for the bespoke formula' (*De Valera and His Times*, ed. J.P. O'Carroll and J.A. Murphy, 2nd ed., 1986, p. 191) and

Ronan Fanning referencing the 'fudge characteristic of other pedantic compromises that studded his political career' (RIA *Dictionary of Irish Biography* at de Valera). De Valera sought, for example, to explain his refusal to go to London for the Treaty negotiations in various ways. And the oath that was an insurmountable obstacle in 1922 turned out to be not such when he later entered the Dáil with his new Fianna Fáil party in 1927. As late as 26 April 2006, in the *Irish Times*, his annoyed grandson Éamon Ó Cuív TD, then a Fianna Fáil minister, claimed that to believe that Fianna Fáil took the oath in 1927 'means that you believe that a person can take an oath without taking the Bible in their hand and swearing by Almighty God to uphold some matter'. It was, he added, 'well-recorded that the Republicans entered the Dáil without taking the oath, and simply signed a book in which the words of the oath were written'.

In April 1922, *Poblacht na h-Éireann – Republic of Ireland* (a paper founded to support de Valera) published a crude satire of the Treaty negotiations that included its narrator proclaiming, 'We'll not have this treaty executed. Let us rather execute the man who signed it for us behind our backs.' In Dáil Éireann, on 27 April 1922, Arthur Griffith described this article as 'a deliberate incitement to the assassination of the plenipotentiaries'. He also quoted then some words attributed by William Henry Curran to his father James Philpot Curran, leading counsel in 1798 for the United Irishman rebel Oliver Bond, when some of the soldiers thronging the court for the state trial clashed their arms and interrupted Bond's defence: 'You may assassinate, but you shall not intimidate me.'

A Lady Sniper

On 6 May 1922, after anti-Treaty forces seized key buildings in Kilkenny city, the *Kilkenny People* reported a remarkable rumour that 'a lady sniper' was among them. It was remarkable because mainly men fought the Civil War. Nevertheless, some women played a role in fighting or promoting it, too. Others were among its civilian victims.

No 'lady' was more vehement in supporting the anti-Treaty IRA than Mary MacSwiney TD, whose brother Terence had died on hunger strike in a British jail in 1920 while Lord Mayor of Cork. In early 1921, Mary MacSwiney made a protracted propaganda tour of the United States for Sinn Féin. Her speech in Dáil Éireann during the Treaty debates was the longest one, and is described by Brian Murphy in the *Dictionary of Irish Biography* as 'a tirade against compromise'. Murphy adds, 'Her opposition even led her to endorse IRA threats against pro-treaty TDs. Apocalyptically, she said the very stones would rise up if this compromise were passed.' MacSwiney attributed the achievements of the Treaty to the efforts of fighters in the War of Independence; she thereby discounted both the great democratic victory of Sinn Féin in 1918, which had marked a definite turning point in public opinion, and the steady work of Dáil

Éireann since that election. Her speech in May 1922 expressed the rationale of absolute republicanism:

> I may say our view was always to take everything belonging to us by force when we could – squeeze it out of England when we could – and snap our fingers at her and use it for Ireland's benefit. Those who have supported the Treaty and because of that support have got certain benefits for Ireland, or think they did – they did not get them because of the Treaty; they got them on account of the War of Independence – should take and use these absolutely for Ireland without any consideration whatever of whether it suits England or whether they should go ahead with the Treaty.

She claimed this was 'entirely the point of view with which those who think of the necessity of preserving the independence of Ireland entered that [Peace] Conference' in 1921, perhaps thus referring to de Valera. Yet it is difficult to see what 'benefits for Ireland' the peace talks had won or could have won that were not dependant on an overall agreement for a Treaty and its enactment by way of the Irish Free State Constitution. MacSwiney blamed the simmering civil strife on the Treaty and not on those taking up arms against the democratic Dáil, 'I have before spoken of the attempt to place the responsibility for the present disturbed state of the country on the shoulders of the Republicans. It will not do. The responsibility rests solely and entirely on the shoulders of those who signed the Treaty and who support it.'

MacSwiney had a strong theoretical point to make about the wishes of the people and British threats of force, 'They say the majority want to accept the Treaty. That is doubtful in spite of the rosy pictures they draw for themselves, because the people in the country have only one great fear and that is the fear of war, "terrible and immediate war," with which England threatened the [Treaty] delegates on the 6th of last December. If that threat of war were taken away, there is no one in this country or in England either who doubts how the people of Ireland would vote.' But the threat remained a reality. Having acknowledged it, she nevertheless embraced civil war as worth fighting:

> We are not going to have that Treaty by a back door, by a front door, by a side door, or by any door. Now I asked the members of the other side before and I ask them again: 'Is the Treaty worth civil war?' I want a straight plain answer to that. They can ask me back, 'Is the Republic, is the independence of Ireland, worth civil war?' And I say: 'Yes, a thousand times yes, it is worth civil war.' The unity and independence of Ireland are as much worth civil war to Ireland, as the unity of the United States was worth civil war to Abraham Lincoln. It is worth civil war and, moreover, the man who declares it is not and believing himself a Republican, lays down his gun rather than fight for the Republic, I call a coward. He has not the courage of his conviction or he is wanting in the faith, just the same as the men who signed that Treaty. We believe that the Republic and the maintenance of the Republic are worth civil war, but is your Treaty worth civil war? Not one of you would dare to say it is.

Members of Sinn Féin on both sides were republicans, with those who supported the Treaty seeing it as a stepping-stone towards their ultimate objective. However, Dáil Éireann could not possibly adopt a republican constitution for the Irish Free State and still abide by the terms of the Treaty.

Hardliner: Mary MacSwiney in London, about six months before becoming a TD for Cork in May 1921 (Courtesy National Library of Ireland [POLF146]). In January 1922, all six women in the 2nd Dáil voted against the proposed Treaty. Of these, Mary MacSwiney alone was subsequently voted into the 3rd Dáil in June 1922. She took the last of four seats in Cork Borough, behind a Labour candidate and two pro-Treaty Sinn Féiners. Four of the others – Kathleen Clarke, Constance Markievicz, Margaret Pearse and Ada English – were defeated, while Katherine O'Callaghan was returned unopposed (and thus without a vote) for Limerick.

British Realities

London loomed over developments in Ireland during the spring of 1922. Although the British handed over Dublin Castle to the provisional Irish government on 16 January 1922, thousands of British troops and their weapons remained in Ireland. They would do so pending full ratification of the Anglo-Irish Treaty by the UK parliament and by Dáil Éireann – ratification that was to come only in late 1922 – and those troops might be deployed at any time if the British decided to intervene militarily again.

The British government was no simple monolith, but an unstable coalition of Liberals and Tories facing high unemployment in England. The War of Independence had been fought to a standstill, not won by either side, and the UK government was under fierce domestic pressure to uphold the Empire and not let down well-organised British and Ulster unionists. In October 1922, the relatively benign Lloyd George would be deposed as prime minister, a change that many blamed at least partly on the Irish troubles. Pressures within the UK Cabinet were exacerbated as strong personalities such as Winston Churchill jockeyed for advantage, and relations were strained between ministers and backbenchers.

In early 1922, the threat of immediate British military action in Ireland that had been made vigorously on the last night of Treaty negotiations in December 1921 was repeated strongly. Suggestions that the Irish Free State, in 1922, might adopt a constitution substantially at variance with the Treaty were as politically unrealistic in the circumstances as de Valera's earlier efforts to pass off his 'Document No. 2' or 'external association' proposal as a plausible alternative to the Treaty. The latter document, produced by de Valera in December 1921, during the bitter Treaty debates, did not simply put forward an adjustment of the proposed terms of the Treaty. It essentially restated fundamental demands that the new Irish state enjoy a status outside the Commonwealth – demands that Britain had absolutely rejected from the outset when Prime Minister Lloyd George met de Valera alone in London in July 1921.

Political divisions at home and in Britain had serious implications for Griffith and Collins. Instead of being free to concentrate without distraction on getting the best deal for frightened Ulster nationalists under the proposed boundary commission, and on setting the Irish economy on a firm foundation for the future, they and their ministers were now embroiled in exhausting meetings in Dublin and London about a Treaty that – as Kevin O'Higgins would soon put it – both the arch-republican Mary MacSwiney TD and the arch-unionist Lord Edward Carson regarded as 'the Great Surrender'. O'Higgins described the provisional government then as simply young men 'standing amidst the ruins of one Administration, with the foundations of another not yet laid, and with wild men screaming through the keyholes' (*Irish Times*, 1 November 1924).

Griffith, Collins and other ministers found themselves obliged to go to London by rail and sea a number of times in early 1922 to defend their position. This meant eleven-hour journeys in each direction, sometimes on rough seas. Meetings in London involving Griffith, Collins and Irish ministers in the first half of 1922 occupied about a fifth of the days between Dáil Éireann's approval of the Treaty and the general election in June.

On 18 September 1922, Minister for Home Affairs Kevin O'Higgins, was to complain in the Dáil that 'Every time we crossed to England to negotiate points consequential on the Treaty [between February and June], things happened here that were meant to be mines under our feet. There was never a time we sat down at the table with the British that wires did not come pouring in of soldiers shot in College Green, or [IRA] raids across the Six-county border or some such incidents that were not calculated to smooth our path and create a better atmosphere.' Newspapers were filled with graphic details of such events – including, on 22 May, the murder of William Twaddell, a unionist member of the Northern Ireland parliament.

Significantly, between 26 May and 16 June – for almost three weeks, as a planned general election in Ireland approached and the Four Courts stayed occupied – senior Irish ministers were tied up in London hammering out a version of the Irish constitution that would be acceptable to both the Irish and the British government as enshrining the Treaty. Yet even then, on 27 May, UK Cabinet Secretary Tom Jones told Lloyd George that 'the more serious trouble' was between nationalists and unionists – the question was 'how to restrain the South and Ulster from flying at each other's throats and plunging into Civil War'.

The finalising of an Irish Free State Constitution was greatly complicated by Collins's attempts to agree with de Valera on an electoral pact that suited both factions of Sinn Féin while also being compatible with the Anglo-Irish Treaty already approved by Dáil Éireann. His attempts finally failed, but his effort significantly strained his previously cordial relationship with Griffith. This, in turn, put even more pressure on the two men as they struggled to hold the centre ground. The armed occupation of the Four Courts from April also proved especially challenging for Griffith as president of Dáil Éireann and Collins as chairman of the provisional government. By the end of August both would be dead, one due to strain and the other due to violence.

Death of the President: Arthur Griffith's remains being removed from City Hall to Dublin's Pro-Cathedral, 15 August 1922. His funeral to Glasnevin cemetery took place the next day. Courtesy National Library of Ireland [Ke167].

OCCUPYING THE FOUR COURTS

On 14 April 1922, hundreds of armed members of the anti-Treaty IRA seized the Four Courts complex in Dublin, along with the adjacent Public Record Office and Four Courts Hotel. Their assault, two days before Easter, during which the assailants held policemen at gunpoint and fired shots, was an unmistakable echo of the rebellion of Easter 1916. Then, republican Volunteers had taken control of the General Post Office and the Four Courts, amongst other key buildings. Now, the occupation in April 1922, led by Rory O'Connor, not only paralysed legal business but also challenged the authority of the provisional government and Dáil Éireann. Other buildings, including the Masonic Hall and Ballast Office, were also seized in Dublin, and there were heavy exchanges of gunfire in the city as anti-Treaty forces tried to extend their control.

The occupiers of the Four Courts clearly intended to resist removal. They dug up soil to fill sacks, with the *Irish Independent* reporting, 'All the windows overlooking the principal thorough-fares were sandbagged, and numbers of law books and what appeared to be bags of papers were also utilised for defensive purposes. Armed sentries were stationed at all vantage points.' Some locals left their homes, 'fearing trouble'. A bakery had its bread taken to feed the garrison.

O'Connor 'declared emphatically' to the *Irish Independent* that the occupation 'should not be taken in any way as a *coup d'état*, nor did it indicate the beginning of a revolution'. His very denial underlined the reality of the threat to the emerging state. His claim that his IRA brigade just needed premises bigger than its current headquarters at 44 Parnell Square ('We simply wanted the place and came here and took it') was not credible. Asked by the Press Association if there were any possible grounds on which an arrangement for preserving peace could be made, O'Connor was adamant, reported the paper, that 'Mr. Griffith and Mr. Collins would have to give an undertaking, and see that it was carried out, that the Provisional Government would not function. He added that the only means he could see of averting civil war was the scrapping of the Treaty.'

Asked how many people were occupying the Four Courts, O'Connor said, 'Quite enough to defend it.' He promised that 'every care would be taken to preserve all documents', but high explosives were stored in one block of the complex and part of the Public Record Office itself was used as a munitions factory.

There were shootings from and at various vehicles carrying armed men in the city. On Easter Sunday night, a clash involving an armoured car of the National Army was followed by a statement from the anti-Treaty side protesting 'definitely and emphatically' that 'an attack on Mr Michael Collins was not in any way intended or contemplated. He happened to be in the vicinity during the incidents at Parnell Square and thus became implicated in the events there' (*Irish Ind.*, 18 April).

Events in Belfast were also putting pressure on the provisional government. On 24 March, a group of Northern Ireland's special police had murdered in cold blood Owen McMahon (a prominent Catholic businessman) and his four sons. Now, on the weekend that the Four Courts was occupied, the lead story in Saturday's *Evening Herald* was not about Dublin but about 'another orgy of bloodshed in Belfast' that had seen five people killed in sectarian violence since Thursday, as well as four members of the Special Constabulary shot, a Catholic church bombed and a Catholic congregation come under fire. It was hard to control the IRA in such circumstances.

That weekend, too, Arthur Griffith went to Sligo to honour a speaking commitment, despite serious tensions in the town due to the presence of pro-Treaty and anti-Treaty IRA units in close proximity to one another. A Sligo alderman who favoured the Treaty said, 'The people would either have to support Dáil Éireann or a military dictatorship.'

The provisional government sent troops to the Shelbourne Hotel and certain other buildings in Dublin, 'as a precautionary measure against possible developments during Easter Week.' Speaking of the Four Courts, one unnamed 'eminent lawyer' complained that 'An enormous number of cases have been pending for many years and are still undisposed of.' This highlighted the disruption caused to commercial and social life by continuing troubles. He made a brave but flawed prediction that 'the Irish administration could take the place by force, but he was certain that they would not do so.' He thought, 'they would be ill-advised in attempting to do so' (*Irish Ind.*, 18 April).

On 26 April, the Catholic hierarchy warned that Ireland was 'on the brink of ruin' and called for matters to be settled by an election and by reason, and not by firearms. The bishops said, 'Like the great bulk of the nation, we think that the best and wisest course for Ireland is to accept the Treaty and make the most of the freedom it undoubtedly brings us.'

Army Councils

On 26 March 1922, an IRA convention met in Dublin; it was convened by Liam Lynch, who had been an active and successful IRA commandant in Co. Cork during the War of Independence and who now opposed the Treaty. The convention was held in defiance of the provisional Irish government. Although IRA headquarters generally supported the Treaty, as many as three quarters of the ordinary IRA membership did not. Delegates to the convention elected an army executive, and Lynch was chosen as its chief of staff. This executive seemed determined to override Dáil Éireann and the provisional government when it deemed this necessary.

'They haven't gone away you know' was a notorious statement made by the Sinn Féin president Gerry Adams in August 1995 when, at a public rally in Belfast, someone shouted 'Bring back the IRA'. The Northern Ireland peace process was faltering at the time. For generations, Irish people have differed about the best way to achieve all-Ireland independence from British or English rule. Some have favoured a peaceful, constitutional response, while others think that only force can ultimately defeat imperial violence and occupation. During periods of extreme tension, such as the 1640s, 1790s and 1840s, both methods have been tried.

In 1918, Sinn Féin's victory in a decisive general election resulted in that movement adopting a two-pronged strategy, with its members not only attempting to achieve independence peacefully at the polling booth but also being prepared to fight as the British repressed the democratic mandate. Arthur Griffith's Sinn Féin movement had been an influential propagandist force for advanced nationalism between its founding in 1905 and the rising of 1916, but it was insignificant in general elections. The fact that it owed its rise in 1918 to the driving force of militant participants in the 1916 rebellion created a paradox. This was that the democratic political movement was inspired by revolutionaries who had acted in the knowledge that the public until then had shown little or no electoral appetite for revolution or even for republicanism. This contradiction created a strained and lasting legacy that was to be manifested in Dáil Éireann on 21 March 1928, when a future Taoiseach, Seán Lemass – then a Dáil deputy of de Valera's new Fianna Fáil party – told the Labour Party's William Davin TD:

> Fianna Fáil is a slightly constitutional party. We are perhaps open to the definition of a constitutional party, but before anything we are a Republican party. We have adopted the method of political agitation to achieve our end, because we believe, in the present circumstances, that method is best in the interests of the nation and of the Republican movement, and for no other reason.

Labour's Thomas J. O'Connell TD here interjected, 'It took you five years to make up your mind.' Lemass – who had been at the GPO during the 1916 rebellion, and whose brother Noel was brutally murdered at the end of the Civil War in 1923 – responded:

> Five years ago the methods we adopted were not the methods we have adopted now. Five years ago we were on the defensive, and perhaps in time we may recoup our strength sufficiently to go on the offensive. Our object is to establish a Republican Government in Ireland. If that can be done by the present methods we have we will be very pleased, but if not we would not confine ourselves to them.

After Dáil Éireann voted by a majority to accept the Treaty in January 1922, not only Sinn Féin but also the Irish Republican Army (the 'old IRA') split internally. Some IRA members tried to remain neutral. And while more of the IRA opposed the Treaty than supported it, this majority was itself divided.

On 15 April 1922, following the occupation of the Four Courts by members of the anti-Treaty IRA, the *Cork Examiner* commented, 'Instead of an anti-Treaty Party, we have a variety of anti-Treaty forces which can be trusted to hamper and negative one another so long as they are given free play.' Indeed, as late as mid-June 1922, Rory O'Connor's faction in the Four Courts clashed over policy with the anti-Treaty stalwart Liam Lynch. Considering him too moderate, it barred him from the Four Courts. He then established his own headquarters across the River Liffey at the Clarence Hotel, although a rapprochement was to follow. Put in mind of the popular Victorian comic operas of W.S. Gilbert, historian Eoin Neeson remarked in his *Civil War 1922–23* (ed. 1989, p.109), 'The situation would have been Gilbertian if it had not been so heavily invested with tragic undertones.'

SUMMER 1922

A barricade of stone or of wood;
Some fourteen days of civil war;
Last night they trundled down the road
That dead young soldier in his blood:

THE BATTLE OF DUBLIN

One might date the start of the Irish Civil War to April 1922. Liam de Róiste – Cork intellectual and Sinn Féin TD – was among those who felt it had already begun by then (Michael Laffan, *The Resurrection of Ireland*, p. 384).

The seizure of the Four Courts by anti-Treaty forces that month threw down a gauntlet that the emerging state could not ignore. Rory O'Connor and the garrison at the Four Courts did not intend to quit unless the Anglo-Irish Treaty was revoked. There had already been shooting elsewhere, including in Limerick and Kilkenny, as the anti-Treaty side seized weapons and buildings. For months, the government held back. Collins attempted a conciliatory 'Pact' with de Valera in May and June, but this was doomed to failure.

It is more usual, however, to date the start of the Civil War to late June 1922, when the provisional government under Michael Collins acted to recover the Four Courts and other buildings held by anti-Treaty forces in Dublin (and did largely recover these in under a fortnight). No Irish government could indefinitely tolerate defiance of the rule of law and democracy, even had UK ministers not been piling added pressure on Collins and Griffith to get a grip by exerting their authority.

A Pact with the Devil?

During the first months of 1922, Liam Lynch, Michael Collins and some other senior veterans of the War of Independence tried to settle their differences peacefully. Collins seemed to have convinced himself that the government could not only accept the Treaty and have a National Army but also somehow adopt a Free State constitution that circumvented the Treaty while letting the IRA function across the border with Northern Ireland.

In May, ten individual officers of the IRA – five from each side – signed a joint proposal. They included government ministers Michael Collins TD and Richard Mulcahy TD on the pro-Treaty side and Tom Hales, brother of the later assassinated pro-Treaty Seán Hales TD, on the anti-Treaty side. The ten acknowledged 'the fact – admitted all sides – that the majority of the people of Ireland are willing to accept the Treaty'. They called for an agreed election with a view to forming a government 'which will have the confidence of the whole country' and for 'army [i.e. IRA] unification' on that basis. They felt 'on this basis alone can the situation be faced'.

On 20 May, Collins and de Valera agreed a pact for such an election. It was a proverbial 'pact with the devil' so far as some of its critics were concerned. Under it, both pro-Treaty and an-ti-Treaty candidates were to stand on the one Sinn Féin ticket, being carefully selected by the party with a view to returning them to Dáil Éireann in the same relative strength as each had in the existing 2nd Dáil that had been formed following the un-contested general election of 1921. As the new voting system of proportional representation required at least three seats in each constituency in order to provide a choice of candidates to whom voters could transfer their preferences, Sinn Féin would now nominate three candidates in a three-seater, five in a five-seater, and so on. If no candidate who was independent or who rep-resented another party stood, then all of the selected Sinn Féin candidates were sure to enter the Dáil as in 1921.

The pact also envisaged a new 'National Coalition' Sinn Féin government in which its 'executive', or cabinet, would include a 'president', or premier, elected by Dáil Éireann, a Minister for Defence whose appointment would be (remarkably for a democracy) subject to the approval of the army, and nine oth-er ministers – of whom five would come from the majority pro-Treaty side and four from the minority. Each side, and not the premier, would choose its ministers – although not their portfolios. The anti-Treaty Sinn Féin ministers might somehow be 'external' and thus not take an oath.

The anti-Treaty side had hitherto striven to avoid an immi-nent general election. This had frustrated Griffith. In the Dáil, on 19 May 1922 – with de Valera, Harry Boland and Cathal Brugha present – he said that if the government did not give voters an opportunity of expressing their opinion on the Treaty, it 'would be condemned for ever as a Government of poltroons'. He added, 'We are making war on nobody. We are asserting the right of Ireland and the Irish people to express their opinion on the Treaty.' The pact now seemed to provide the people with just such an opportunity and to provide de Valera with a path back to power, and even perhaps with a settlement that might sideline the Treaty. However, it also affirmed that 'every and any interest' was free to nominate candidates, and this time – to the chagrin of some Sinn Féin TDs who had never had to compete for their seats – others stood for election. Voters had a choice in some constituencies.

In practice, the Sinn Féin pact panel consisted of sixty-five pro-Treaty and fifty-seven anti-Treaty candidates. Of those who were pro-Treaty, fifty-eight were elected (of whom seventeen had been unopposed). Of those anti-Treaty, thirty-six were elected (of whom sixteen had been unopposed). Thus, Sinn Féin overall filled 94 of the 128 Dáil seats.

Of all first preference votes, anti-Treaty Sinn Féin won only 22 per cent (half a percentage more than the Labour Party did). Pro-Treaty Sinn Féin won 39 per cent. All of the candidates who were not members of Sinn Féin in fact accepted the Treaty, and these won a greater total of first preference votes than either of the Sinn Féin factions. Among hardline anti-Treaty deputies who lost their seats were Liam Mellows, Constance Markievicz and Erskine Childers. Childers received just five hundred votes, finishing last of ten candidates in his constituency.

Seventeen out of eighteen Labour Party candidates were elected. Given that the eighteenth fell short by only thirteen votes, it is quite possible that Labour's Patrick Hogan would have dislodged one of the Sinn Féin panel in de Valera's own constituency of Clare had he, too, run. Hogan and three other non-panel candidates had somehow been persuaded to withdraw at the very last minute (it is said that the election official even turned back the hands of his watch to give Hogan more time to decide by the deadline to withdraw). Seven deputies from a new Farmers Party, and ten independents – including four for Dublin University – were also returned to the Dáil. Nevertheless, eighty-four years later, de Valera's grandson Minister Éamon Ó Cuív TD dismissed as a total misrepresentation the notion that 'the Treaty was endorsed by the electorate in June 1922' (*Irish Times*, 26 April 2006).

The anti-Treaty side felt betrayed by Collins. Shortly before the election, he made a speech in Cork urging people to 'vote for the candidates you think best of'. In his analysis of the election and of press coverage of that speech, the political scientist Michael Gallagher has rejected a later suggestion that Collins was widely seen at the time as repudiating the pact (*Irish Historical Studies*, Sept. 1979).

Only on the day of the election was the draft of the new Irish Free State Constitution, as finally agreed with the British, published. It clearly reflected the Treaty agreement. One historian suggested in 1980 that the only explanation for Collins ever believing that the alternative draft pact constitution discussed with de Valera could be squared with the Treaty (if he really did so) was that 'his legal advisers were breathing the rarified air of constitutional theory, untainted by political realities' (Joseph M. Curran, *Birth of the Irish Free State*, p. 204).

Meanwhile, 'shocking crimes' and a sectarian 'orgy of violence' were consuming Northern Ireland (*Irish Times*, 22 May 1922). In Dublin, a coalition government comprising the two Sinn Féin factions was not formed, although between them they had a clear majority of Dáil seats – arguably having been helped on both sides by the Sinn Féin pact to maximise their vote. The 3rd Dáil was due to meet for the first time on 1 July. Dublin then was a civil war battleground. The provisional government 'prorogued' (suspended) parliament by proclamation. By the time that the Dáil next met, on 9 September 1922, Collins would be dead. So, too, its president Arthur Griffith. W.T. Cosgrave TD took on both of their mantles, as chairman of the provisional government and president of the Dáil respectively. The proroguing of Dáil Éireann for two months was said to be a necessary emergency measure, being strongly urged by Collins. Critics have claimed that it reflected an authoritarian, if not dictatorial, tendency on his part and was a denial of democracy.

Better Days: Michael Collins addressing Speaker (Ceann Comhairle) Eoin MacNeill TD in the 2nd Dáil, at its temporary chamber in Dublin's Mansion House, August 1921. Beside him on the sofa is Arthur Griffith. Left of Griffith in an armchair is Éamon de Valera, reading a document or paper. Returned to the 3rd Dáil in June 1922, Collins and Griffith were dead and de Valera was on the run by the time that it first sat in September. Courtesy National Library of Ireland [Ke220].

Retaking the Four Courts

On 28 June 1922, the new National Army began shelling the Four Courts. The government's patience had run out in the face of a usurpation of its authority to determine national policy. That this, in fact, was what the garrison itself thought it was attempting became even clearer that day when Rory O'Connor, Liam Mellows and other IRA commanders at the Four Courts issued a proclamation describing their resistance as 'the continuance of the struggle that was suspended by the truce with the British'.

The political context had been made more difficult on 22 June by the assassination in London of Henry Wilson, a former serving head of the British Army and prominent advisor to the new Northern Ireland government. This was, as Kevin O'Higgins wrote, 'simply another barrel of oil on the flames'. The British prepared a plan to attack the Four Courts themselves but thought better of it. Instead, they pointed out to the Irish that the Treaty could not possibly proceed unless the occupation was ended and order prevailed in Ireland. Irish ministers had suffered armed defiance and attacks since February but now acted forcefully.

Within two days, the principal buildings of the Four Courts complex were destroyed, and its remaining garrison arrested.

The Press Association reported that 'The Irregulars, who fought with a grim desperation in face of a bombardment which increased in intensity and effect as the day wore on, must be given credit for the courage they displayed.' Nonetheless, it was clear that 'the Irregulars' were defeated even before the 'terrific blast' witnessed at the Four Courts shortly after noon on 30 June. The next day, newspapers reported that this was caused by the occupiers' main ammunition dump blowing up; the eruption was so theatrical in its force that photographs of it are imprinted on Irish public memory as the very emblem of a desperately destructive civil war:

> The explosion was of tremendous violence. Observers saw a great flame leap into the air, the atmosphere for some distance around became dark, and a thick pall of smoke hung over the dome [...] Debris was showered far around, and charred documents of national records were picked up in the streets a mile away. The roadway near the Four Courts was blocked with shattered masonry and broken tramway wires lay scattered about. Free State troops to the number of about thirty were wounded, and some forty civilians and Republicans are stated to have been injured (*Cork Ex.*, 1 July 1922).

A temporary truce was agreed for the removal of casualties. With ambulances already hard pressed across the city, twenty doctors drove to the Four Courts in a coal dray and removed the injured.

There would be bitter recriminations around the questions of whether or not the government was acting 'at the direction of our hereditary enemy' England (as the garrison's proclamation put it), and whether or not the anti-Treaty forces were to blame for the destruction of the Public Record Office along with its invaluable trove of ancient documents. The British had certainly pressed to have action taken to establish order in Ireland, so that they could extricate themselves from the emerging Free State and get on with implementing the Treaty, but the provisional Irish government itself could not have permitted the occupation to continue indefinitely and simultaneously retained credibility. The fact that it needed to get two field guns and some ammunition from the British Army to do the job, lacking appropriate ordnance of its own, was a detail that did not change that basic political reality. By this time, some of the anti-Treaty forces themselves had agreed to accept British rifles furnished to the provisional government – ones that Collins was willing to hand over to the anti-Treaty IRA if it, in turn, would deliver some of its older untraceable weaponry to the northern IRA, which was embroiled in Northern Ireland's sectarian strife.

According to Michael Fewer, in his *Battle of the Four Courts* (London, 2018), the Irish Army's gunners who took charge of the artillery used it carefully and were by no means reckless when shelling the building. He also finds that the occupiers' main ammunition dump was located neither inside the Public Record Office nor in the main Four Courts building. Nonetheless, the conflagration resulted in the loss of many legal papers of current and great historical importance, as well as the collapse of the dome of the Four Courts.

After the blast, the remaining members of the occupying garrison – by that stage thought to number about one hundred – surrendered. About four o'clock that Friday afternoon, the garrison marched out to be taken prisoner. The 'gallant soldiers of the Irish Republic', as they described themselves, were given drinks, food and cigarettes, and chatted with their captors. Some produced a large tricolour flag and sang the 'Soldier's Song'. They lined up and were marched away to jail along the quays:

> Thus ended the principal phase of the historic Dublin battle, which gave rise to such terror, tension and uneasiness. It is a matter of conjecture at the time of writing if the surrender of the Four Courts will represent a complete cessation of hostilities. Sniping of a general character continued throughout the city long after, and while the citizens are greatly composed at the Four Courts result, there is yet fear that the fighting and sniping which really formed the greatest menace to those having business in different thoroughfares, may continue for some time (*Cork Ex.*, 1 July 1922).

The Irish government had used force to end the occupation of the Four Courts and assert its authority, won at great effort through both the War of Independence and democratic elections. Ministers may have felt reassured about their decision to act decisively when news came of the burning down of a Protestant orphanage at Ballyconree in Clifden, Co. Galway that same weekend – 'by order of the Republican [anti-Treaty IRA] Headquarters as reprisal for inmates' loyalty', according to a naval officer quoted in parliament by Winston Churchill on 4 July 1922 (*Hansard*). This was one of a number of ostensibly 'republican' actions during the Civil War that can seem at least partly ethnic or sectarian, no matter how justified by reference to informing or spying. The British immediately dispatched a destroyer to evacuate staff and children from Clifden, a sign of their willingness to intervene if deemed necessary.

'Death before Dishonour'

Dublin's main thoroughfare, O'Connell Street, was badly damaged during the 1916 Rising. Now, again, in early July 1922, artillery blasts rocked its buildings as the National Army moved on from the Four Courts to secure a block at the north end held by anti-Treaty forces that included Oscar Traynor and Cathal Brugha. This block encompassed the Granville, Gresham and Hammam hotels. The National Army also ejected anti-Treaty forces from a number of individual buildings around the city, including Elvery's and Eason's on O'Connell Street itself. In his *Civil War in Dublin* (2017), John Dorney suggests that some of the claims about the anti-Treaty forces – that they abused Red Cross flags and white flags to smuggle weapons and even to kill soldiers on the other side – were correct.

Before the Civil War, the Gresham Hotel had been a favourite haunt of some IRA leaders, including Collins. Now, de Valera and his closest advisors, including Austin Stack, were installed at the Hammam Hotel. Brugha and Stack, as Cabinet ministers, had sided with de Valera in December 1921 when the Cabinet split 4–3 on the agreement for a Treaty. Hardliners even before then, neither man chose to go to London to participate in the Treaty talks.

A final bombardment of the hotel block took place on 4 July, leaving it in ruins. Towards the end, Oscar Traynor and most of the fighters escaped from the Hamman Hotel, with de Valera and Stack also clearing off. About twenty fighters remained, including Cathal Brugha – that 'indomitable spirit', as the title of a welcome new biography by Daithí Ó Corráin and Gerard Hanley reminds us he was known. The devout Catholic son of a Protestant nationalist and an austere man of principle, Brugha had fought heroically in 1916. He was appointed the temporary first president of Dáil Éireann in 1919, while Britain continued to intern de Valera and Griffith.

Under impossible conditions, Brugha finally ordered his men to surrender but he himself decided not to do so. On 5 July, he emerged into the street with a revolver in his hand and was shot once. It looked very much like 'death-by-cop', as Americans call it when a suicidal person deliberately provokes their own killing. 'Death before Dishonour' had been 'an unchanging principle of our national faith' invoked earlier by the Four Courts garrison before it surrendered. Brugha left behind a wife and six children.

Had the single bullet not hit an artery in his thigh, Brugha might have been captured and imprisoned. In the event, he died in hospital two days later. In America, the leading Irish republican Joseph McGarrity drafted a message of sympathy. He praised 'Cahil's [sic] unbending spirit' and promised 'His death will be avenged and his principles vindicated' (McGarrity Papers, NLI MS 17,525/350). Ó Corráin and Hanley reflect on how this 'often misunderstood figure' was 'propagandised after his death'. His portrait hangs opposite that of Arthur Griffith in the hall of Leinster House, home to Dáil Éireann.

Unruly Prisoners

On 7 July 1922, an anti-Treaty garrison occupying Skeog House in Donegal surrendered; however, they set fire to Letterkenny Courthouse when taken there as prisoners. Many of the men were from Northern Ireland. That same week, the *Irish Independent* reported that crowds in Dublin were conversing with republicans jailed at Mountjoy by shouting to them. It understood that guards had been told 'to fire on any persons loitering near the prison, or endeavouring to get into communication with the prisoners'.

Were members of the Four Courts garrison either prisoners-of-war or political prisoners, with more rights than ordinary criminals? The National Army stated that 'their point of view seems to be that it is right for them to wreck, burn, shoot, commandeer and use force in every form, but that the use of force against them is wicked and tyrannical.' It claimed that the prisoners demanded 'every comfort', and when refused, 'these people who a few hours previously had hung out the white flag before they had lost a man, became exceedingly aggressive and unruly.'

Harry Boland Shot

On 31 July 1922, Irish Army troops trapped the prominent anti-Treaty republican Harry Boland in a hotel in Skerries, Co. Dublin. Boland's father, James, had been a member of the Fenians who died aged just 38. The Boland family ascribed his death to a brain cyst caused by a fight with opponents of the great Irish leader Charles Stewart Parnell.

Harry Boland himself was a member of Sinn Féin, and a close friend of Michael Collins before the Treaty was agreed. He was shot and seriously wounded by the troops in the raid at Skerries. Aged 35, he expired next day at St Vincent's Hospital, Dublin. This was around the corner from a nursing home where Arthur Griffith would die less than a fortnight later. Unsurprisingly, allegations about the circumstances of Boland's death generated controversy.

Given Boland's dedication, energy and skills in the service of the revolution before the Civil War, his passing was a tragedy. He was well regarded and popular. Boland frequently represented Sinn Féin interests in the United States and Britain between 1919 and 1921.

Many attended his funeral procession, mourning a man whom the historian David Fitzpatrick has described in the *Dictionary of Irish Biography* as 'one of the most genial, attractive, yet impenetrable of Irish revolutionaries'. Jack Yeats expressed the general dismay at Boland's loss in two paintings: *A Funeral* and *A Lament*.

There are conflicting accounts of why Boland was in Skerries that night, and about the circumstances of his arrest. Was he armed or unarmed? Was he set up? Did he resist arrest? Did the troops mean to kill him? As when Michael Collins died later that month, rumours would long fester and circulate about the possible level of malice behind his killing. It is unlikely that such rumours could ever be entirely dispelled or resolved. It was the Civil War itself that destroyed both men. The deaths of many former friends and even brothers were inevitable once hostilities erupted.

On 2 August, Collins passed St Vincent's Hospital. He wrote to his and Boland's mutual friend Kitty Kiernan:

> My mind went into him lying there and I thought of the times together, and whatever good there is in any such wish of mine, he certainly had it. Although the gap of 8 or 9 months [since the Treaty split] was not forgotten – of course no one can ever forget it – I only thought of him with the friendship of the days of 1918 and 1919. They tell me that the last thing he said to his sister Kathleen, before he was operated on, was 'Have they got Mick Collins yet?' I don't believe it so far as I'm concerned and, if he did say it, there is no necessity to believe it (*In Great Haste*, ed. León Ó Broin, p. 219).

Collins concluded, 'I'd send a wreath but I suppose they'd return it torn up.'

A War of Friends: Michael Collins was at Croke Park to throw in the ball for the Leinster Senior Hurling Final on 11 September 1921, when Dublin beat Kilkenny. With him was his friend Harry Boland TD (left), who himself had played on the Dublin hurling team in an All-Ireland senior final in 1909. Both men would be dead within a year, on opposite sides in the Civil War.

Pádraig de Búrca wrote in the *Irish Independent* (12 September), 'It was nothing new to us to see Harry Boland in Croke Park, with his camán [hurley stick]. Many a time has his unerring stroke brought victory to the Faughs [a Dublin GAA club]. But when Michael Collins had a few preliminary shots before he started the match yesterday we realised that he, too, had handled a hurley before [...] for five minutes the fifteen thousand spectators saw him no longer a hunted fugitive or a Minister of Finance, but a schoolboy at play.' Also there, in a bowler hat, was James Nowlan of Kilkenny, long-term GAA president.

Collins signed this photo for a leading Irish republican in America, Joe McGarrity. Two days after it was taken, Harry Boland met British Prime Minister Lloyd George in Scotland; he was then acting as Éamon de Valera's go-between in setting up the Treaty negotiations in London that ended in December 1921. Photo courtesy National Library of Ireland [NPA JMG 11].

GRIFFITH'S BROKEN HEART

On 12 August 1922, Arthur Griffith, president of Dáil Éireann, collapsed and died at a nursing home on Leeson Street, Dublin, to which his doctor had insisted he be admitted for rest. He had been unwell for a while, passing some nights at government buildings under guard because ministers were threatened by sniper fire when they emerged. A lifetime of struggle had exhausted him.

Just days before Griffith's death, his doctor and personal friend Oliver St John Gogarty arranged for an influential Irish-American, James Duval Phelan, to visit the 'very ill' Griffith. Phelan – the former mayor of San Francisco, and US Senator for California until 1921 – had not slept soundly in Dublin since his arrival, as the city's roofs resounded to sniper fire. He wrote that he found Griffith 'a nervous wreck' then, 'He was obsessed with the idea that, in the cruel vendetta disgraceful and abhorrent to him, he was the next in turn to be sacrificed. He, the originator of the Sinn Féin movement, whose intellectual prowess was the pride of his countrymen, there miserably dying in an hospital.'

Summoned urgently by the nursing home, Gogarty found Griffith lying on his back at the top of the stairs. Someone had made a vain effort to counteract a cerebral haemorrhage, subsequently certified as the cause of his death. In September, the

Chicago Tribune and some English newspapers ran a rumour that Griffith had been poisoned, claiming his body was exhumed and that people were arrested. His close personal friend Walter Cole contradicted this, and the relevant cemetery authority stated that Griffith's body was not exhumed. In 1937, in his memoir *As I Was Going Down Sackville Street* (pp. 188–9), Gogarty commented that 'the poison that slew Griffith was envy and jealousy and calumny, which can be deadlier than prussic acid, and, what is more mortal to a martyr, ingratitude':

> He had not the armour with which I, for one, was invested, be it irony or motley. His sincerity was a bow and his belief an arrow which, if deflected, slew his faith [...] When I think of what Griffith set out to acquire and the character of the man, which was indeflectible, his achievement of the 'Treaty' is a conquest which excelled all that he set himself to accomplish twenty years before. His 'concessions' were conquests. His camp followers may have expected more loot, but the General's plan of campaign cannot be decided by the avarice of the hangers-on or the *vivandières*.

Lloyd George was represented at Griffith's funeral by the senior Downing Street official Thomas Jones. Jones told his wife that he went afterwards to have lunch at half past two in Jammet's, Dublin's leading French restaurant, before going out to the annual Horse Show at the RDS in Ballsbridge, 'There was Society and a gathering of many beautiful Irish women and magnificent horses. We saw the jumping for an hour or more.' Harry Boland had sometimes dined at Jammet's before his death. Clearly the city was not entirely devastated by Civil War.

When Griffith died, a sealed envelope he had given to James

Montgomery to mind in case of such an eventuality was opened at government buildings. It rallied the public, 'Let the people stand firm for the Free State. It is their national need and economic salvation. Love to the Irish people, to all my colleagues and friends' (*Irish Times*, 26 Aug. 1922).

Both Harry Boland and Michael Collins admired Griffith. 'Hasn't he made us all?' asked Boland. Collins reportedly called him 'the father of us all'. Griffith had launched Sinn Féin in 1905, as a 'movement' rather than simply as a political party, intending it to unite advanced nationalists. The weekly papers that he edited, when not suppressed by the British, inspired a generation. Notably, on 14 August 1922, the leading anti-Treaty organ *Poblacht na h-Éireann* described Griffith as 'the greatest intellectual force stimulating the tremendous national revival' and praised his 'almost single-handled' combat of 'political torpor' before 1916. People have often said he died of a broken heart due to the outbreak of civil war.

Bruce Chatwin once wrote that 'history aspires to the symmetry of myth' (In *Patagonia* [New York, 1988], p. 95). Griffith was pragmatic and asymmetrical, an awkward fit for the historical narrative ('myth') of Irish political parties. He was more radical economically than the future Fine Gael, a reproach to the abstraction and extremism of Fianna Fáil's future founder Éamon de Valera, too moderate for later Sinn Féin and (although called a 'friend' by the socialist James Connolly) not progressive enough for leftists and liberals. In her *Commemorating the Irish Civil War* (2003), Anne Dolan has a chapter titled 'The forgotten President: the awkward memory of Arthur Griffith'.

AUTUMN 1922

We are closed in, and the key is turned
On our uncertainty; somewhere
A man is killed, or a house burned,
Yet no clear fact to be discerned:

COLLINS DEAD AT BÉAL NA BLÁ

Michael Collins died in an anti-Treaty ambush at Béal na Blá, Co. Cork on 22 August 1922. One newspaper reported, 'The fatal news of the killing of General Michael Collins [...] fell like a bombshell on Dublin. Consternation reigned supreme amongst the people of all ranks of life.' It also noted an attempted assassination of him earlier in that week, in Dublin, with a bomb thrown and shots fired (*Sligo Champion*, 26 August). Collins had been elected chairman of the provisional Free State government in January 1922. In July, as civil war raged, he took command of the National Army, and was frequently seen driving through Dublin almost unattended – 'his buoyant, breezy, eagerly alert appearance was greatly admired,' according to the same report. His last formal public appearance was at Arthur Griffith's funeral. Now Dublin learnt of his death, as the *Sligo Champion* also wrote:

> On Wednesday morning at 7 o'clock the citizens were startled by the newsboys calling out 'Stop Press' editions of the daily newspapers. In the suburbs the newsvendors appeared in considerable number and their resonant calls brought people to the doors to secure the papers. The idea of such a

catastrophe did not seem to present itself to any mind. The first notion was fed by a rumour which prevailed on Tuesday in the city. It was thought that the news that caused this early commotion was the surrender of the irregular leaders. But amazement sat on every face when the papers were opened and the tragic truth became known. People were seen standing in the streets and roads and on the doorsteps gazing at the news. It had an almost stupefying effect [....] He became to them once more the well-beloved daredevil darling of the war [of independence]. 'Poor Mick Collins' was the ejaculation heard on all sides. 'God have mercy on him.'

John Lavery, the Belfast-born artist who made portraits of Collins and other Irish and British Treaty negotiators in London in 1921, now produced two memorable paintings: one showing the body of Michael Collins laid out in state, with a Christian crucifix and an Irish tricolour on top of it; and the other with his closed coffin at his funeral Mass submerged in a sea of mourning by church and state.

So who killed Collins? Was it his anti-Treaty ambushers (almost certainly), or one of his own? Had the British some hand in it? Was de Valera directly responsible? Rumours swirled but would never bring him back. Had he lived, he might have become a great leader of Ireland, or perhaps gone wrong as an Irish Mussolini. Now, the two chief Irish architects of the Anglo-Irish Treaty were both dead, within three weeks of each other. With them went an irreplaceable fount of knowledge of British attitudes, expectations and statements during the negotiation of a peace deal that their surviving colleagues had yet to ratify in the form of a Free State constitution.

Guerrilla Clashes

On 9 September 1922, the 3rd Dáil met for the first time. Minister for Defence Richard Mulcahy TD spoke of the 'great Chiefs' Griffith and Collins: 'Since the last Dáil separated we have lost the two people who were the leaders, and to whom we looked, as the leaders of the future – one of them the greatest sower who lived in Ireland while we have been here, and the other the greatest reaper the country has ever had.' He said that implementing the Treaty would 'save our Country from outside enemies', but that the Dáil must 'carry out means for defeating internal enemies, or very, very bad friends of our Country [...] who are endeavouring, with whatever motives, to destroy a very big portion of that freedom which their own particular efforts helped us to get.'

Hopes that the ejection of anti-Treaty IRA forces from buildings that they held in Irish towns would quickly lead to the end of the Civil War were dashed. The anti-Treaty forces resorted to a kind of guerrilla warfare in order to wreck Ireland's infrastructure, including bridges and railways, and to make the emerging state ungovernable. The spring of 1922 had been marked by a measure of reserve, and even cordiality at times. Summer had seen some prominent anti-Treaty leaders quickly captured and jailed. The period from autumn into deep winter became increasingly bitter. Members of the National Army engaged in official and unofficial reprisals, including executions, while their opponents threatened to kill anyone actively supportive of the provisional government.

Resistance to the government seemed strongest in Munster, with the troops of the National Army landing by boat at Passage West in Cork and Fenit in Kerry, to avoid ambushes. Cork City was captured in August when General Emmet Dalton and other Free State forces arrived with artillery and armoured cars on board the SS Lady Wicklow – a vessel built in 1895 for the City of Dublin Steam Packet Company.

Events in Kerry took a particularly sour turn. In September, a 'series of shocking outrages' in Killarney was reported. These included armed and masked men calling to the homes of six female anti-Treaty sympathisers and rousing them from bed before painting their bodies green (which presumably means they were stripped). Next day, hundreds of anti-Treaty volunteers captured the town of Kenmare from Free State forces taken by surprise. Tom and John O'Connor of the National Army, natives of Kenmare, were in their own home. Reportedly unarmed, the two officers were shot dead there. Kenmare was soon recaptured, however, and an attempt by the anti-Treaty side to repeat its success, at Killorglin, failed. As many as two dozen anti-Treaty attackers were killed at Killorglin.

A few days later, it was reported that an anti-Treaty force at Ballina, Co. Mayo attacked that town while at least half of the National Army garrison there was in the cathedral, unarmed and at a Requiem Mass for a comrade who had been killed. Two civilians (a young girl and a cattle-dealer) were among the dead that day. So it went wearily.

'Considerate' Censorship

During 1922, the government introduced military censorship. On 20 September 1922, the editor of the *Irish Times* wrote that, so far, the censor had done his work 'considerately and well'. But the editor was concerned about recent orders to omit passages relating to the treatment of prisoners and other matters.

The anti-Treaty IRA had its own means of censorship. On 17 February 1922, it had seized and burned copies of the *Freeman's Journal* and *Irish Independent* that reached Cork containing an article written by J.J. Walsh, the postmaster-general, that it did not like. In March 1922, in an armed raid, it smashed the presses of the *Freeman's Journal*. In October 1922, it threatened fines and 'much more drastic action' against editors who used the term 'irregular' for the anti-Treaty side or enclosed in quote marks the title or rank it gave its members.

Words were significant. A government minister of 1922 wrote years later, 'There was actually reluctance at the time to describe the armed opponents of the Anglo-Irish Treaty as *rebels*, not on legalistic grounds, but because Irish history had practically made the word rebel a term of approbation [praise]. Therefore the word Irregular was invented by someone – I think Piaras Béaslaí' (Ernest Blythe, *Irish Times*, 19 Nov. 1968; the word is actually found used earlier for troops outside an established army). Blythe added, 'No one was reluctant to describe the struggle as Civil War.' In fact, this appears not to have been the case at the outset, as Mary MacSwiney TD told the Dáil on 17 May 1922:

> In an interview given to the Press yesterday, Mr. Collins said that there would be no civil war in Ireland; that only a police measure would be necessary. Mr. Collins is evidently fast following in the footsteps of [the British] Macready, Tudor, Smyth, Hamar Greenwood and all of that ilk. They always refused to call the war that was being carried on in Ireland a war at all. That is why they sent the Black-and-Tans and used them more than soldiers. We all know that they did not want to dignify it with the name of war. So. Mr. Collins does not want to dignify the name of our opposition to the Treaty with civil war. It will only be a police measure.

The government instructed editors to use the word 'irregular' to designate anti-Treaty IRA fighters. In late 1922, the anonymous author of a pamphlet wrote that the government had also ordered that the terms 'forces' and 'troops' were not to be used for 'irregulars', but 'bands' or 'bodies' instead; the army of the new state, on the other hand, must always be referred to as the 'Irish Army', the 'National Army' or simply 'troops' (*The Pen is Mightier than the Sword*).

Articles, photographs and films relating to the Civil War had to be sent to the office of Piaras Béaslaí, Army Publicity Director (censor), for vetting. He also employed people in the main postal sorting office to open suspect letters, including those to newspapers in Belfast and London. For its part, the anti-Treaty side sometimes ordered editors to publish items or submit content for approval in advance of publication (e.g. see *Freeman's Journal*, 28–9 April 1922; *Irish Ind.*, 24 July 1922). During the first two weeks of May 1922, the anti-Treaty IRA suppressed the *Clonmel Nationalist* and held one of its reporters prisoner.

The official censor might order changes to reports of court cases or inquests. The *Dublin Evening Mail*, for example, got into trouble when it carried a full report of the inquest into the death of Harry Boland. It had quoted references to the barrister James Comyn acting for the anti-Treaty 'army executive council' and repeated the words 'murder' and 'unlawful' used during proceedings. In another inquest, into Muriel Bruton's ostensibly accidental shooting in the back on her way to the theatre, a reference by her father to 'three or four Free Staters' proved problematic. James Whitehead, a chief sub-editor, complained to John Murphy, his editor at the *Dublin Evening Mail*, that the censor had deleted 'Free Staters' and substituted 'soldiers', 'I cannot reconcile myself to the policy of changing the statements of counsel or witnesses (especially when reported in the first person) and I think it would safeguard the newspapers if, instead of changing passages to which he objects, the Censor deleted them entirely.' The editor himself told Béaslaí on 9 August 1922 that 'we have always endeavoured to ease things by deleting all matter that seemed against the national interest or likely to be officially censored' (Piaras BéaslaI Papers, NLI MS 33,915).

Responding to an enquiry from McConnell's Advertising Service, the censor explained he had stopped the publication of an army invitation to tender for a supply of coffins as it 'might have a bad effect from the propagandist point of view and could be quoted by the irregulars as showing that we expected a long and bloody struggle'.

The Freeman's Journal

[Estd. 1763] IRELAND'S NATIONAL NEWSPAPER [Estd. 1763]

DUBLIN THURSDAY MARCH 30, 1922

SUPPRESSED AGAIN !

What Greenwood, Macready, Strickland, the British Army, the Auxiliaries and the Black and Tans failed to do the patriots of the seceding section of the I.R.A. have done.

RATHER THEY THINK THEY HAVE DONE IT

But they have failed; and they will continue to fail

Because the "Freeman's Journal" has fought for the freedom of the plain Irish people.

Because it sought to ensure that they should decide their own destinies in their own way.

The Black and Tans of Suffolk Street determined to put it out of existence.

Close on a hundred of their followers, flourishing revolvers, raided our offices soon after midnight.

With sledges they smashed every single machine.

They sprinkled the premises with petrol.

Then the heroes of the Documentary Republic set them alight.

The "Freeman's Journal" does not appear in its usual form this morning.

BUT IT APPEARS.

And so far as it is humanly possible it will continue to appear.

Even if only in a sheet the size of this.

And it will continue to say what it chooses.

It will expose tyranny in whatever garb it shows itself.

Whether in the khaki of the British or the homespun of the mutineers.

Whether in Dublin Castle or in Suffolk Street.

The paper that has fought for Irish Liberty so long will not be silenced.

Nor will the Irish people be terrorised out of their rights.

They have fought for freedom; Not for the rule of the mutinous bully.

Means of Censorship: A special news sheet circulated by the *Freeman's Journal* when anti-Treaty forces smashed its printing presses in March 1922. Courtesy Kenny Family Collection, Dublin City University Library P2/1/3/15.

DE VELERA: 'I WAS SO FOOLISH'

Two months after Éamon de Valera resigned as president of Dáil Éireann in January 1922, he set up a political grouping for anti-Treaty deputies, Cumann na Poblachta. This described itself as 'the Republican Party'. However, a pact with Collins would see him and his supporters stand again under a Sinn Féin pact banner in June 1922.

As matters spun out of control later in 1922, de Valera found himself sidelined by the anti-Treaty IRA fighters. This became public knowledge when letters between him and an anti-Treaty TD, Charles Murphy, fell into the hands of the Free State government. He wrote in one, 'Rory O'Connor's unfortunate repudiation of the Dáil, which I was so foolish as to defend even to a straining of my own views in order to avoid the appearance of a split, is now the greatest barrier we have.'

On 27 September 1922, in Dáil Éireann, Minister for Defence Richard Mulcahy TD put these letters in context. He quoted de Valera as writing, 'The position of the political party must be straightened out. If it is the policy of the party to leave it all to the army, well then the obvious thing for members of the party to do is to resign their positions as public representatives. The present position is that we have all the public responsibility, and no voice and no authority.' De Valera, as quoted, also confessed, 'Even if we had the allegiance we have not the military strength to make our will effective, and we cannot, as in the time of the War with the British, point to authority derived from the vote of the majority of the people.' He saw the writing on the wall, 'We will be turned down definitely by the electorate in a few months' time in any case.' Mulcahy explained that de Valera was proposing, as a way out of his dilemma, that the anti-Treaty army executive take effective control:

Then he [de Valera] continues: 'This is the course I have long been tempted to take myself; and were it not that my action might prejudice the cause of the Republic, I would have taken it long since. Our position as public representatives is impossible.' [...] on the 14th September a meeting was held at which were present Count Plunkett, Miss MacSwiney, Tomas O'Donoghue, Cathal O Murchadha, Mrs. Clarke, Derrig, Countess Markievicz, J. O'Mahony, Frank Fahy, Dr. Jim Ryan, Brian O'Higgins, and they agreed that the military would take over control and that they as a party – that is, a political party – would co-operate. The Army position was stated: 'Intend putting policy before us and taking over control, we to work with them.'

Mulcahy added that members of the public were looking to their leaders for hope and some leaders were here saying that they have absolutely no right to talk as public representatives. He added firmly:

We shall have to deal with the situation which is around us as if there was no past. Charged with the organisation of the country and the setting up of its administration we have a certain group of people, who, by murder and burnings and every type of destruction, are trying to ruin our people. We certainly shall have to deal with these people when they have taken up that attitude. If there are people who are soft-headed about it, and they include public representatives, too – we cannot blame them very much because we have been very slow in realising the facts ourselves – some of us at any rate [...] Where we say that sentences of imprisonment and death must pass upon those who are killing the country we are simply stating what the ordinary civil machinery of the country would do if it were there.

The minister denied that the government's response to continuing violence was in any way 'done in a spirit of revenge'.

Eventually, in October 1922, de Valera formed what was styled a republican government. Claiming legitimacy against the government chosen by Dáil Éireann, his 'government' tried to give his claims credibility and to acquire funds collected earlier in the United States for an envisaged Irish republic. As civil war dragged on, de Valera's difficulties produced characteristically paradoxical formulas to appease both public opinion and the anti-Treaty IRA leaders. For example, according to historian Michael Hopkinson in 2004, de Valera let it be known that he thought Liam Lynch's support for widespread reprisals against key pro-Treaty personnel would alienate the public but yet backed Lynch's determination to attack Britain. 'It appears that violence, which might well imperil the lives of non-combatants, was more acceptable to de Valera in Britain than in Ireland,' wrote Hopkinson (*Green against Green: The Irish Civil War*, p. 235).

THE PUBLIC SAFETY BILL

On 27 September 1922, Dáil Éireann ratified and approved, by 48 votes to 18, certain powers that the National Army felt it required as 'a matter of military necessity'. Most controversially, under the 'Public Safety Bill', as these special powers became known, military courts now had jurisdiction to impose not just fines or jail terms but even death sentences. Dozens were to be executed on foot of the measure. In response to it, the anti-Treaty IRA threatened deputies who supported the motion. Acting on its threat, it would shoot dead Seán Hales TD in early December.

The special courts could try someone for attacking the National Army, damaging any public or private property, or possessing without proper authority an explosive or firearm or other lethal weapon or any ammunition for such firearm. They also had jurisdiction, vaguely, over 'the breach of any general order or regulation made by the Army Authorities'. Each court had to include at least one person certified to have legal knowledge and experience.

On 27 September, Cosgrave told the Dáil that armed opposition to the National Army was really an attempt to overthrow an elected parliament and 'a direct challenge to the authority of the people':

One of the reasons put forward for this armed opposition is that the Treaty was accepted under duress, and the question naturally arises as to whether or not the people had a right under the circumstances to accept the Treaty [...] the minority in the country had no right to say that the people were bound to accept war, or bound to accept their opinions, when their opinions were not the opinions of the majority of the people.

Cosgrave outlined the harm being done by the Civil War:

It restricts trade, it attempts to destroy the industry of the nation, it delays the progress of public administration, it destroys life, damages public and private property, it shakes public security, it defames our nation, injures the people's health, and endangers the future generation as it helps to destroy the people's peace; it delays the departure of the British troops, and it has given rise to new propaganda which violates divine and human law.

Cosgrave said that from the beginning the government had hoped that it 'might possibly be able to crush this rebellion without resorting to such stern measures of justice [...] but the absolute disregard of life and of suffering that is evidenced by the continuance of the irregular attacks plainly indicated to the Government that protection is due to their soldiers.'

Nonetheless, the Labour Party voted against the measures. Its leader Thomas Johnson TD quoted Cosgrave as saying two days earlier, 'The liberty of the person is inviolable, and no person shall be deprived of his liberty except in accordance with law.' Johnson now told the Dáil:

It is the evidence that cannot be produced in a public Court that is going to be produced before a Military Court, where personal spleen and spite may very often affect the situation; and it is on that evidence, that kind of evidence, that a man may be transported, that a man may be executed, that a man may be imprisoned for as long as the Court decides. Who will defend that honestly? I challenge any lawyer to do it.

On 3 October, in tandem with the introduction of special powers, the government offered a full amnesty and pardon to any anti-Treaty insurgent who would surrender their arms and go home on or before 15 October 1922.

The Public Safety Bill was passed partly to dissuade Free State forces from taking matters unofficially into their own hands, as they were rumoured to have done in the case of the anti-Treaty Brian MacNeill. Brian, the son of pro-Treaty Minister for Education Professor Eoin MacNeill, was found dead in Sligo in late September. Nonetheless, unlawful executions by state forces continued to occur. These included, on 6–7 October, the killing of three teenage members of the anti-Treaty IRA who were arrested pasting up handbills in Dublin. King's Counsel Michael Comyn, for their families, told an inquest that Eddie Hughes, Brendan Holohan and Joe Rogers had decided to help 'a little girl named Jenny O'Toole, who had been employed by the Irish Republican Army in posting up ordinary Republican placards. She had been abused and ill-treated by some people, mud having been flung at her' (*Freeman's Journal*, 10 October). Their bodies were found on the outskirts of Dublin, riddled with bullets.

ANGUISH AND EXCOMMUNICATION

On 10 October 1922, the Irish Catholic hierarchy issued a pastoral letter condemning actions of the anti-Treaty side and calling on young men to avail of the government's amnesty that month. Its letter, stronger even than one it had issued in April 1922, first appeared in newspapers. However, the bishops soon released a slightly revised text. This was not least, as Patrick Murray has demonstrated in a critique of the pastoral, to remove an adjective the bishops had used when expressing their horror at reading of 'the many unauthorised murders recorded in the Press', which had implied a concept of '*authorised* murders' (*Oracles of God: The Roman Catholic Church and Irish Politics, 1922–37* [Dublin, 2000], pp. 72–8; 425–30). Murray found no public episcopal condemnation of state failings during the same period, but some bishops privately made known to the government their concerns about executions.

The hierarchy began its pastoral of 10 October by proclaiming that 'The present state of Ireland is a sorrow and humiliation to its friends all over the world':

> Our country that but yesterday was so glorious is now a byword before the nations for a domestic strife as disgraceful as it is criminal and suicidal. A section of the community,

refusing to acknowledge the Government set up by the nation, have chosen to attack their own country as if she were a Foreign Power. Forgetting, apparently, that a dead nation cannot be free, they have deliberately set out to make our Motherland, as far as they could, a heap of ruins. They have wrecked Ireland from end to end, burning and destroying national property of enormous value, breaking roads, bridges and railways, seeking by this insensate blockade to starve the people, or bury them in social stagnation. They have caused more damage to Ireland in three months than could be laid to the charge of British rule in so many decades [...]

With feelings of shame we observe that when country houses and public buildings were destroyed the furniture and other fittings were seized and carried away by people in the neighbourhood. We remind them that all such property belongs in justice to the original owners and now must be preserved for and restored to them by those who hold them.

The bishops noted that the anti-Treaty side was conducting what it called a war, 'but which in the absence of any legitimate authority to justify it, is morally only a system of murder and assassination of the National forces.' They added:

They ambush military lorries in the crowded streets, thereby killing and wounding not only the soldiers of the Nation, but peaceful citizens. They have, to our horror, shot bands of those troops on their way to Mass on Sunday; and set mine traps in the public roads and blown to fragments some of the bravest Irishmen that ever lived. Side by side with this woeful destruction of life and property there is running

> a campaign of plunder, raiding banks and private houses,
> seizing the lands and property of others, burning mansions
> and country houses, destroying demesnes and slaying cattle.

Even 'worse and sadder than this physical ruin', thought the bishops, 'is the general demoralisation created', with young lives 'utterly spoiled by early association with cruelty, robbery, falsehood, and crime […] our hearts are filled with the bitterest anguish.' The hierarchy believed 'The long struggle of centuries against foreign rule and misrule has weakened respect for civil authority in the national conscience.' It rejected the idea that the legitimate authority in Ireland was somehow not 'the present Dáil or Provisional Government', adding, 'A Republic without popular recognition behind it is a contradiction in terms.'

The hierarchy warned that, 'All those who in contravention of this teaching participate in such crimes are guilty of grievous sins, and may not be allowed to Confession nor admitted to Holy Communion if they persist in such evil courses.' To members of a fighting force largely composed of proud Catholics, this was excommunication and it hurt. The bishops stated that 'no oath can bind any man to carry out a warfare against his own country in circumstances forbidden by the law of God,' and they insisted that people had a duty 'to assist the government in every possible way to restore order and establish peace'. The hierarchy rejected any suggestion that it was politically biased or wished to help one political party, 'If it were true, we were unworthy of our sacred office.' The anti-Treaty side made representations at a high level against this pastoral, but to little or no effect.

WINTER 1922

An affable Irregular,
A heavily-built Falstaffian man,
Comes cracking jokes of civil war
As though to die by gunshot were
The finest play under the sun.

Munster Sailing: General Emmet Dalton (extreme right) with Free State soldiers on board the SS Lady Wicklow in August 1922 (Courtesy National Library of Ireland [HOGW3]). A veteran of the British Army in the First World War, Dalton fought in the Irish War of Independence and was at Béal na Blá with Michael Collins when the latter died. He was made Director of Military Operations for the new National Army. Uneasy at the government's decision to execute anti-Treaty prisoners, Dalton resigned in December 1922. He was later a film producer and co-founded Ardmore Studios, Bray, Co Wicklow.

Dalton was aged just 24 when this photograph was taken, a graphic reminder of the youth of many who fought in the Irish revolution.

The 77 : Orders of Frightfulness

They died on 17 November 1922, shot by a firing squad in a Dublin prison. The four men had been arrested in late October, after the government's amnesty for anti-Treaty combatants had expired. James Fisher had been employed at Ruddell's cigarette factory in James Street; Richard Twohig, at the Inchicore Works of a railway company; both Peter Cassidy and John Gaffney, in the electric lighting department of Dublin Corporation. The latter two were local commanders of the anti-Treaty IRA (*Irish Ind.*, 18 Nov. 1922).

According to the *Belfast Newsletter*, 'The announcement in the Dublin evening papers yesterday that four young men, presumably Republicans, had been executed after being condemned to death by a Free State military court, for having been in possession of revolvers created a great sensation'. The writer thought that this was 'first because there had been no hint that the sentences had been imposed, and; secondly, because the public frankly believed that the Provisional Government would never have the courage to execute any of its prisoners [under the Public Safety Bill]'.

It has been estimated that there were seventy-seven officially sanctioned executions of anti-Treaty republicans by shooting between 17 November 1922 and 2 May 1923 (eighty-one when four other particular executions are sometimes included). The deaths of 'the 77' men, listed in 1937 in Dorothy Macardle's formidable *The Irish Republic* (pp. 1,021–23), have been bitterly remembered.

On 27 September 1922, as deputies debated the Public Safety Bill, W.T. Cosgrave made his government's case for special military courts in place of the usual administration of justice, 'There is no justification in any way that I know of, or that is subscribed to by any body of people in the country, for these ambushes on our troops. I think that will be admitted. It will also be admitted that, in the present state of society, verdicts would be rather difficult to get, and then any body of malcontents [...] could hold up the administration and say: "It is impossible for you to get verdicts, because we have swept away the means, the normal circumstances, by which these verdicts are got."'

Cosgrave continued, 'These people have got to learn that if they so agitate against society and declare war on society, there is an alternative method of bringing them to justice, and that is the method that is outlined here. So far, the military authorities have not executed one single person, and the war is now almost three months old.' He said that he had always objected to the death penalty but that there was now no other way of which he knew 'in which ordered conditions can be restored in this country, or any security obtained for our troops, or to give our troops any confidence in us as a Government'.

Later on the day of the executions in November, the Labour Party leader Thomas Johnson expressed shock in the Dáil at the sudden news, 'unless there is some very much fuller explanation and justification for the execution of four men contained in that bald announcement I prophesy a deep revulsion of feeling against the Army and against the Government.' He thought that

'The possession of a revolver does not justify the execution of a man, lawfully or unlawfully.' General Richard Mulcahy TD replied to him frankly:

Anything that will shock the country into realisation of what a grave thing it is to take human life is justified at the moment […] we regret that we have had to face the responsibility of dealing with the situation that calls for measures as plain and as drastic as those measures. The men who were executed this morning in Dublin, were found on the streets of Dublin at night, carrying loaded revolvers, and waiting to take the lives of other men. It was because those men were found under such circumstances, with such intent, that it was necessary to execute them here this morning.

Mulcahy had succeeded Collins as commander-in-chief of the army while retaining his portfolio as Minister for Defence. His residence had been bombed and shot up on 2 November, with one of the attackers being killed. He now added, 'We are faced with eradicating from the country the state of affairs in which hundreds of men go around day by day and night by night, to take the lives of other men.' He was scathing:

We have people in the country proclaiming that their aim and their object, the immediate aim and object before them, is to unite the people of Ireland, and the way they do it is they put arms into the hands of young men and mid-dle-aged men and they send them out to take the lives of other Irishmen […] There are people who take it to themselves and to their immediate neighbours and comrades to settle the difficulty of land acquisition, if not land purchase, in Ireland, and their policy is, as disclosed in their orders to subordinate officers, 'Give him a bullet', and we are faced with dealing with a proposition like that.

Four more men died on the day after the executions of 17 November. Nevertheless, the Press Association reported that on this occasion, the anti-Treaty activists killed themselves at Inchicore when conspiring to ambush National Army soldiers by preparing a mine. There was 'a huge flash' as it prematurely exploded.

Then, on Monday, 20 November, two men were charged before a military court with having shot dead Joseph Hanrahan, a soldier in the National Army, on the same day on which the first four of the 77 had died in Dublin. Also that Monday, the UK parliament considered the ongoing threat within Ireland to the Anglo-Irish Treaty agreement. The Irish government, if not the public, had to bear in mind political realities, including what the British might yet take upon themselves to do in Ireland if order was not maintained. The chaos in Dublin potentially posed a threat to the United Kingdom.

In addition to both the lawful if unpalatable executions of men who committed specific offences under the Public Safety Bill and various unlawful executions by both sides out in the field, there were, in December 1922, the four 'authorised murders' of Rory O'Connor and his colleagues as will be considered later – men imprisoned before the Public Safety Bill was passed and simply shot in reprisal for the assassination of Seán Hales TD, with which they had no proven connection. All of the executions, whatever their nature or rationale, exacerbated the bitterness between old friends and former comrades.

Few of the 77 executed around Ireland by official authority of the Provisional Government were senior or even mid-ranking anti-Treaty leaders. One of the few exceptions was Erskine Childers (below). Their deaths generally were calculated to deter their compatriots – or, in Voltaire's quip of 1759 concerning a particular French execution, 'to encourage the others'. In 2006, a sympathetic account of these mainly little-known men, *Seventy-seven of Mine Said Ireland*, by Martin O'Dwyer, was published in Cashel, Co. Tipperary.

In late 1922, Liam Lynch reacted viscerally to the officially authorised executions of the first of the 77. While demanding 'evidence' of a potential target's wrongdoing from his IRA members, he immediately authorised them to kill members of military courts or courts martial and anyone who mistreated republican prisoners.

An extant copy of another order indicates that on the day of the first four official executions, he also sanctioned shooting on sight members of the provisional government, but none was subsequently shot (Ernie O'Malley Papers, NLI 10,973/11). These were part of a series of what became known as his 'orders of frightfulness', which targeted people who had voted for 'the Murder Bill' (i.e. Public Safety Bill) and their homes, as well as the houses of civilians who actively supported the Irish Free State and approved of its policy of executions. The first instance of his order to kill being carried out in the case of elected representatives appears to have been the assassination of Seán Hales TD on 7 December 1922.

CHILDERS EXECUTED

On 24 November 1922, Erskine Childers, a leading anti-Treaty activist who had lost his Dáil seat in the June general election, was executed by firing squad. His proven offence consisted of the possession of a small pistol, once given to him as a keepsake by Michael Collins. 'It is 6 a.m.', he wrote to his wife Molly Osgood on the morning of his execution, 'you will be pleased to see how imperturbably normal and tranquil I have been this night and a.m. It all seems perfectly simple and inevitable, like lying down after a long day's work.' He and his guards of the previous evening had exchanged courteous words before they went off duty. They requested souvenirs, and he gave them a few books and signatures. He told his wife, 'So we, "children of our Universal Mother", touch hands, and go our ways in the very midst of the horror of this war of brothers' (*Sinn Féin*, 23 Nov. 1923).

In 1921, Childers had been a divisive presence when de Valera made him a political secretary to the Treaty delegation in London. During 1922, as a propagandist on the anti-Treaty side, he infuriated the pro-Treaty Irish government. It also believed that in August 1922, Childers and some others damaged one transatlantic cable at Valentia, Co. Kerry and attempted to cut a second, but this assertion was later contested. There is a surviving file at the Irish Military Archives, dated early November 1922, in which the Office of the Director of Intelligence admits to the adjutant general that the file does not 'supply anything which could form the basis of a charge' against Childers (Military Archives, DOD/ A15296-E4; *Dáil Éireann* debates, 11 Sept. 1922).

Childers was arrested on 10 November 1922 at Glendalough House, Co. Wicklow, 'A shooting fight – in the passage outside my door, when taken, would have endangered two women there, and that is why I did not use my pistol and only tried to force my way through,' he told his wife.

Educated in England and graduating from Cambridge, Childers fought for Britain in the Boer War, and worked as a loyal civil servant before adopting the Irish cause. Although he became one of the fiercest critics of the Treaty, his efforts to be accepted as a member of the IRA in Cork and Kerry were rebuffed during the Civil War. He was a magnet for suspicions of double-dealing, being disliked by some who feared that he was a British agent, disdained by others who regarded him as the stooge of a devious de Valera during the Treaty negotiations of 1921, dismissed as a 'damned Englishman' by Griffith in Dáil Éireann (an uncharacteristic outburst that Griffith was said to have regretted), and rumoured during 1922 to be favoured by the anti-Treaty IRA chief of staff Liam Lynch to supplant de Valera as leader of the anti-Treaty political movement.

His purpose in London during Treaty talks was set out in a confidential letter that de Valera sent his republican backer Joe McGarrity in New York in December 1921. De Valera was eager to represent the Treaty delegates as having strayed off message. Apologising to McGarrity that 'there is so much of the ego in this', de Valera contemptuously described Griffith and Collins as 'bait' intended by him to lure Lloyd George into concessions

rather than to conclude a deal, and he referred to the two delegates Gavan Duffy and Éamonn Duggan as 'mere legal pad-
ding'. Childers, however, was 'an intellectual republican' sent
to give Robert Barton (the fifth of five delegates, and his near
cousin and close friend) 'added strength' as 'a retarding force'
(Sean Cronin, *The McGarrity Papers*, pp. 107–11). Yet even Barton seems to have recoiled from Childers then, a fact not widely
known at the time but to which Childers's own diary attests.
Barton was to claim, in 1954, that Griffith, Collins and Duggan
had said 'the most terrible things' to get him to sign a deal that
night. He did not mention then that his close cousin Childers
applied great pressure on him to get him *not* to sign. Paradoxically, this was counterproductive, as Childers himself wrote on
the day the agreement was signed, 'Privately today R.C.B. [Rob-
ert Childers Barton] said that my allusion to [Childers' wife]
Molly's support for refusal to sign last night made him sign –
deciding element – because her name reminded him of thousands
of homes to be ransacked' (Childers diary, TCD MS, f. 88v, f.
102; BMH WS 979, pp. 41–2; italics added here).

Childers wrote from jail before he died that 'my treatment
while under sentence here has been very considerate and courteous – commandant, officers and men of the guard and all.
Nothing to complain of; on the contrary.' But his widow tried
in vain to recover certain items that Childers had on him when
arrested, including a gold watch, silver cigarette case and gold
cuff-links that were 'of a special and sacred value to her' because they were originally her father's. The Military Archives
(DOD/P/387) show that she wrote to the authorities on 26 July
1923 that she had not made the losses known because she was
'anxious not to add anything to the prevailing bitterness'.

A MONSTROUS, INHUMAN THING

In Dáil Éireann on 28 November 1922, George Gavan Duffy TD demanded an explanation for the execution of Erskine Childers. Gavan Duffy had been one of the five plenipotentiaries who negotiated the Treaty in London in 1921, when Childers served as a secretary to that team. As one of the agreement's signatories, Gavan Duffy had told the Dáil on 21 December 1921, 'My heart is with those who are against the Treaty, but my reason is against them, because I can see no rational alternative.' A barrister, he subsequently resigned from the provisional government when it wound up the revolutionary Dáil courts against his wishes, but he would later serve as president of the high court of the Republic of Ireland.

As he spoke in November 1922, Gavan Duffy paid tribute to Childers and criticised the manner of his trial and his execution. He said, 'Erskine Childers was a great Irishman, and I emphasise that because he was an Irishman, not merely in law, but also in fact, and because it has been so unscrupulously denied up and down the country, unscrupulously, or ignorantly, if you like. He was an Irishman in fact, because he was born of an Irish mother, and brought up in this country, and consecrated his life in later years to the independence of Ireland.' Gavan Duffy then focused on the circumstances of the trial:

Remember that you had, first of all, the trial *in camera*, so secret that all the public were allowed to know on the first day of the trial was contained in this brief announcement from the Press Association: 'The trial of Mr. Erskine Childers was opened before a Military Court at Portobello; the nature of the charge is not disclosed. Mr. Childers is defended by Counsel. The proceedings were private.' Even the name of his counsel must not be given and the crime with which he is charged must not be made known to the public. That is the kind of thing which is the acme of folly for any Government – this extraordinary secrecy, this unnecessary secrecy, which seems to pervade the dealings of the authorities with these strange tribunals [...] Not only that, Erskine Childers, who cared nothing about his own life but wanted to save the lives of others, applied for a *Habeas Corpus* [challenging his detention] [...] ah! it was a humiliating thing for the Government to be compelled to rely upon the fact that there is a war [...] It was a humiliating thing for the Government to be brought to that, when the case all along is that this is not a war, because if it is a war it is clear that you must treat your prisoners as prisoners of war. Is not that ordinary logic? These are various minor circumstances. They would be major circumstances in any other case; they are minor circumstances in a case like this where the fundamental thing that is wrong is that this man is executed on that charge when he had that pistol in what was virtually his own home.

Cosgrave, as president of the Dáil, responded sharply to Gavan Duffy, dismissing him as being 'afraid of his shadow'. Cosgrave said:

What we are concerned about is saving this country from weak-kneed people like the Deputy who has just sat down – saving them from that lack of moral courage which has almost submerged the country and in regard to which we are going to do our duty in our time and in our day [...] We knew from the very commencement of this struggle that a scheme of assassination was in the minds of the people opposed to us, and that day after day their Press reeked with incentives to their unfortunate dupes to commit that assassination. They have not succeeded so far.

Cosgrave appealed to 'a higher law than the law of nations, and that is the Law of God' and claimed that his government was trying to uphold it:

We could publish every scintilla of evidence given at these Courts to satisfy the morbid curiosity of Deputies like the Deputy who has just spoken, but it is not desirable to do it; it is not in the public interest to do it. We are as good judges of the public interest as the Deputy. We were in public life before him, and if God spares us we will be in public life after him. And if there is any constituency in this country in which he would like to challenge me on that I will take him up. Deputy Gavan Duffy was not here when the execution of the four poor citizens of this city [James Fisher and others] was discussed. It was not worth his while. He had to wait for an intellectual to be executed. This is a democratic country and the people responsible for bringing these unfortunate dupes to their doom must take the responsibility for their action.

Members of the Labour Party criticised the manner of military executions; Cathal O'Shannon TD, for example, remarked in particular on the failure to notify families in advance that their loved ones were to be shot:

> It is a monstrous, inhuman thing that when a man is about to be executed that neither his relatives nor the general body of the people are to know that he is to be executed. But after an hour or two, or six or eight hours after the execution, the Military authorities will turn round and send a letter or something like that to the nearest relation of the execut-ed person saying that duly – at 6 or 7 o'clock or whatever the time was – that that person was executed. There is only one parallel for inhumanity of that kind and that was the inhumanity of the British Command in the European War when a printed postcard was sent notifying the execution of certain soldiers in France and on other fronts. Nothing in my experience has been more inhumane than this.

At the same time, O'Shannon made it clear that he did not approve of the anti-Treaty violence, 'Now, as I said before, I am not going to justify the actions of those who are in arms against the Provisional Government. I do not think on any ordinary grounds of reason that they can be justified. I do not justify them and I condemn, as much as I deplore, ambushing, assassi-nation or anything like that.' When trying to occupy a moderate middle ground, Labour Party deputies such as O'Shannon were caught between a rock and a hard place.

ROADS AND RAILWAYS WRECKED

Browsing through Irish newspapers for 1922 and early 1923, one finds many reports of violence and destruction, of shootings and bombings, and of the injury or death of civilians caught in crossfire. Some injuries were collateral, but much damage to property was deliberately calculated to make the emerging state unmanageable.

On 29 November 1922, General Richard Mulcahy TD placed before Dáil Éireann a captured document revealing the strategy of anti-Treaty forces, who feared by then that they were losing the Civil War. They were conducting a campaign against Ireland's infrastructure of roads, railways, bridges and waterworks. Intended to disrupt effective government, this caused significant economic harm. With republican gangs roaming the countryside and a Free State soldiery accused of drunkenness, civilians were terrified. In addition to pro-Treaty and anti-Treaty violence, some were using the banner of the republic to settle old scores, grabbing land, robbing for their personal gain and engaging in sectarian attacks against Protestant unionists north and south.

Among those killed was P.J. Cosgrave, an uncle of W.T. Cosgrave TD. The latter had succeeded Michael Collins as head of the provisional government. P.J. Cosgrave died when he grabbed

the revolver of one of four men robbing a family pub and gro-
cery shop. Dr Tom O'Higgins, father of the Minister for Justice,
died in similar circumstances when raiders called to his house
in Stradbally, Co. Laois, possibly intent on burning it. In early 1923, anti-Treaty forces destroyed the houses of thirty-seven
Free State senators.

Retreating to his late medieval tower house in the remote
countryside of south Co. Galway, where he composed 'Meditations in Time of Civil War', W.B. Yeats did not escape the
chaos. An adjacent little ancient bridge was blown up by remarkably courteous anti-Treaty forces: 'They forbade us to leave
the house, but were otherwise polite, even saying at last "Good-
night, thank you," as though we had given them the bridge,' he
wrote.

In the Dáil on 29 November 1922, Mulcahy quoted the order to members of the anti-Treaty IRA that had come into the
government's possession. This envisaged a systematic and con-
tinuous destruction of all communications: road, railway, canal,
telephone, and telegraph infrastructure:

> 'Roads: These are to be made impassable at as many points as
> possible. Bridges are to be destroyed by explosives wherever
> this can be done, roads to be trenched, blocked with trees
> or masonry, telegraph poles, or other material available. In
> certain localities the roads may be flooded by breaking down
> the canal banks. Barricades, to be of any use, must be placed
> at frequent intervals at one section of the road [...] Railways:
> To be destroyed by every possible way. Bridges to be destroyed
> by explosives. Small stations to be attacked and burnt. Where
> station buildings cover the track they should be destroyed so
> as to block the permanent way. Station coverings are generally

supported on cast-iron columns, and one or two blows with a heavy sledgehammer will generally knock these to pieces. By blocking the railway line by means of the station buildings at two points, protection will be afforded to a demolition party working between these two points. Before the obstructions are cleared and an armoured train reaches them the demolition party will have had time to completely wreck the track […] If a train is held up, it need not be run into an obstruction to wreck it. Four men with sledges can destroy the wheels of all the carriages and the locomotive in a few minutes. By destroying the wheels on the inner side only, some carriages can be thrown across the other track. The carriages should be soaked with paraffin and set on fire, and the mechanism of the locomotive battered to pieces.'

Some of the above operations were expected to take place every week, in each area. On the evening of Friday, 8 December, for example, an anti-Treaty force held up the mail train from Mayo at Liffey Junction near Dublin. It was, as one newspaper reported, 'a rather lonely locality, close to the Banks of the Royal Canal […] At night it is generally a deserted spot.' Armed men had been operating around the district 'with some energy' for the previous two or three months – the railway line and the railway traffic claiming most of their attention, according to the paper. On 8 December, armed men compelled passengers to leave their carriages and to enter a compartment at the rear of the train. They then ordered the driver and fireman to put on steam so that they could set the train in motion, before forcing him from the engine. Some of the anti-Treaty force sprinkled petrol on cushions and elsewhere in the empty carriages, setting them on fire, while others tried to uncouple the rear compartment containing the passengers. When they found themselves unable to uncouple it from the burning train, they simply abandoned the attempt. They then started the engine.

A Press Association report continued, 'Realising that the passengers were being carried along with the burning train the rebels shouted to them to jump for it. This they did before the train was fully under way, and many of them sustained severe bruises.' The train travelled in the direction of Broadstone Station. According to the *Irish Independent*, however, the driver of the train had managed to reboard it as it glided out of Liffey Junction station, and due to his efforts, the train was brought safely into a siding at Broadstone. Four or five people unable to jump out were 'in a state of collapse' before being rescued. The *Freeman's Journal* reported that a little girl named Mullaney, from Ballina, was injured in the head, 'her teeth being knocked out', while a man from Ballina was 'seriously injured'. Ultimately the flames failed to catch hold completely, and 'there was only a smouldering fire in the carriages when the train stopped.' The *Freeman's Journal* speculated that the attack was designed in the same fashion as a spectacular earlier one, 'only that it differed in being more audacious and reckless'. A previous incident at the same place had involved the letting loose of a powerful goods engine, 'which ran a three-mile course, burying itself in the North Wall and causing enormous destruction'. The largest of Ireland's railway companies estimated (*New History of Ireland*, vol. vii, 50) that in 1922, its line alone had been damaged in 375 places, forty-two engines had been derailed and fifty-one bridges had been destroyed.

'Buckshot' Shot

On 7 December 1922, in the very week that the Irish Free State formally became a constitutional reality, Seán Hales TD was shot dead. He died when leaving Dublin's Ormond Hotel by horse-drawn cab to attend Dáil Éireann. According to the *Tipperary Star*, 'Poor Hales' and his brother Tom had been 'amongst the best fighters and the sturdiest sufferers during the Black and Tan terror'. His exploits included leading an assault on two truckloads of British soldiers during the War of Independence.

Hales was ostensibly killed on the orders of the anti-Treaty IRA. His assassination as a serving member of Dáil Éireann occurred just two days after the UK parliament ratified the new Irish Constitution – thus giving legal effect to the Anglo-Irish Treaty – and the day after the 3rd Dáil first sat officially as the lower chamber of the new Irish Free State's Oireachtas (parliament).

Under the headline 'Dublin Horror', the *Cork Examiner* reported, 'Seán Hales, T.D., the famous Co. Cork leader in the war with England, was shot on his way to the Dáil yesterday, and died in hospital. At the same time Mr Patrick O'Malley, T.D., was wounded, but likely to recover. Both had seen active service in flying columns [of the IRA] in the South and West.'

It is thought that Pádraig Ó Máille ('O'Malley'), deputy chairman or 'speaker' of Dáil Éireann, may have been the main target. Had the attack not happened, both men would have been present that evening when Dáil Éireann elected half of the sixty members of the first-ever Irish senate.

At an inquest on 8 December, Lance-Corporal Frederick George Haines said he was on Ormond Quay in charge of a British armoured car. The last of the British Army had not yet left the Free State, and would not do so for another nine days. Haines saw civilians scattering. Two men were running with revolvers in their right hands. It was too late to turn the armoured car after them, so he jumped out, drew his revolver and called on them to halt. When they ignored him, he fired a warning shot over their heads. They kept running, and Haines felt he could do no more.

Hales was a veteran of the 1916 Rising. The *Cork Examiner* also described him as 'the man who kept the [IRA] men together in South and West Cork, and was in many ambushes.' It added a poignant fact: Seán 'was a brother of Tom Hales, a prominent Irregular [i.e. anti-Treaty] leader, who was recently arrested.' The brothers had been close friends of Michael Collins, although Tom Hales took part in the ambush that killed Collins. In early 1922, as their comrade Michael O'Donoghue later told the Bureau of Military History, each brother addressed passionate meetings about the Treaty:

> A big crowd listened but there were many interruptions and hecklings. Prominent among the hecklers were the young I.R.A. men and officers from the Bandon quarters, including myself. Seán Hales was known to all there and the I.R.A. men there were all known to him being his own comrades.

His main case for the Treaty was based on the argument, which I first heard here from the lips of Seán Hales, and which I was to hear ad nauseam from every Treaty advocate for years after, that 'What was good enough for Michael Collins was good enough for me'. Collins's prestige, personality and status were projected into the whole campaign for acceptance of the Treaty and, without the magic of his name, the Treaty would never have been ratified and implemented. The verbal exchanges at this meeting between Seán Hales and the I.R.A. hecklers were in a very friendly strain, jocular and witty rather than critical, and Seán, a very jovial man, revelled in the repartee and seemed to get a great kick out of it. (BMH WS 1,741)

O'Donoghue added that a speaker named Murphy aroused hostility. It was 'an egotistical performance in marked contrast to Seán's homely modesty and amiable attitude':

Then, suddenly, the wagonette used as a platform by the speakers burst into flames. It had been set afire by a disorderly hooligan element who took advantage of the excitement and the confusion. Murphy and the other Treaty speakers got very indignant, but Seán kept his sangfroid and his joviality, an attitude which all, especially we of the I.R.A., appreciated. Seán stayed on the burning vehicle until the flames reached him, then, throwing up his hands in mute helplessness, he jumped down amid the crowd and mingled with his I.R.A. comrades who continued to watch the dying embers of the wagonette with mixed feelings. Their uppermost reaction was that 'Damn it all, this is hardly good enough for poor old "Buckshot" (Seán Hales's beloved nickname).'

Shortly afterwards, another meeting was held, this time by those opposed to the Treaty. The principal speaker was Tom Hales:

> Tom, a very serious, solemn man, who had survived barbaric torture while in the hands of the Essex Regiment in Bandon Barracks, and who abhorred compromise and expediency, showed in simple yet eloquent logic how hollow was the so-called Treaty and how disastrous would be the consequences of accepting and working it. A man in the crowd asked: 'How is it that you are so much against the Treaty and your brother Seán voted for it?' I'll never forget Tom's answer: 'If the first pair of brothers whom God Almighty put on earth quarrelled to the point of murder, is it any wonder that the two of us should disagree?' All were impressed by Tom's simplicity and burning sincerity and I thought of my R.I.C. [Royal Irish Constabulary] brother, at that time somewhere in Tyrone, between whom and me were such tremendous differences of ideology where Ireland and Irish Freedom was concerned.

Denis Lordan told the bureau (WS no. 470) that in June 1921, shortly before a truce was declared in the War of Independence, Seán Hales had led the IRA Volunteers who burnt Castle Bernard, the residence of the earl of Bandon. They had gone to kidnap the elderly Lord Bandon as a bargaining chip, but he could not be found. Hales reportedly said, 'as the bird had flown we will burn the nest'. Lord Bandon then appeared, witnessing the destruction of his home. He was held hostage until British authorities guaranteed that IRA volunteers in Cork prison would no longer be executed. There is a sad irony in the fact that the Irish government responded to Hales's assassination in 1922 by summarily executing four anti-Treaty prisoners.

Authorised Murder

At 3.30 a.m. on 8 December 1922, less than twenty-four hours after Seán Hales TD was assassinated, guards at Mountjoy Prison woke four anti-Treaty inmates and told them they were to be shot at dawn. Rory O'Connor, Liam Mellows, Richard Barrett and Joseph McKelvey were not tried, even in accordance with the government's drastic Public Safety provisions for military courts, and were not convicted of any specific offence. They were leaders of the Four Courts garrison that had surrendered six months earlier. Mellows wrote to his mother at 5.00 a.m. that 'we were informed that we were to be "executed as a reprisal"' for the murder of Hales. Their fellow prisoner Brighid O'Mullane was an executive member of Cumann na mBan:

> On our way back from the early Mass we heard one of the criminal prisoners who was always calling out to us, shouting something about executions, and when we returned to our cells the breakfast bread, butter and tea had not arrived as usual, and I, from my previous prison experience, knew that this foreboded nothing good, as whenever executions were taking place no outsiders, not even the milkmen, were allowed in. Then in a short time we heard a volley of rifle fire from what

seemed to be a number of guns, and then the *coup de grace* from revolvers. Sheila and I scrambled up as best we could to the cell window, clinging to the bars, and all we could see was a number of soldiers with rifles, evidently coming back from the scene of the execution. (BMH WS 485)

Richard Barrett, from a Munster farming family, had actually been a close friend of Seán and Tom Hales during the War of Independence. He opposed the anti-Treaty policy of killing public representatives. Joe McKelvey, from Ulster, was the son of a member of the Royal Irish Constabulary. He was one of the Four Courts garrison responsible for the capture of J.J. 'Ginger' O'Connell, deputy chief of staff of the new 'National Army' – as the pro-Treaty forces soon became known. That kidnapping had greatly exacerbated tensions. Rory O'Connor was the son of a solicitor and was educated by the Jesuits at Clongowes Wood College, Co. Kildare. An engineer, he was a close personal friend of Michael Collins's before strongly opposing the Treaty. O'Connor was also best man at the wedding of Kevin O'Higgins TD, now Minister for Home Affairs in the Irish government. On the day the prisoners died, O'Higgins told Dáil Éireann:

It is all right to say these are honest men. It is not a question of their honesty. They have not a monopoly of honesty, and a man can be personally an honest man and be a greater danger to the community in which he lives than a mad dog in a playground full of children [...] we have simply to face the fact that certain men, or a certain combination of men, are garrotting this country, and we have to deal with those men by the only means that we know of and with the only weapon that is to our hand. It would be criminal on our part to allow this country to be garrotted for want of using that weapon sufficiently strenuously.

O'Higgins denied vehemently that there was any question of vengeance or 'hot blood' in the decision to execute the four, 'Personal spite, great heaven. Vindictiveness! One of these men was a friend of mine.'

Liam Mellows was born in an English military barracks, the son of an Irish soldier in the British Army. In 1895, his parents moved to Ireland. Christian and socialist, he was close to James Connolly, who was executed in 1916. Mellows was prominent in the IRA in the west of Ireland during the War of Independence. Some believe he was executed alongside the three others, who came from Ulster, Leinster and Munster respectively, to send a clear message to all four provinces of Ireland. The territorial imperative of these and other state executions during the Civil War has recently been analysed by Bill Kissane (*Social Science History*, 45 [2021]). An idealist, Mellows became a hero of the anti-Treaty republican left. Yet as Conor McNamara's published selection of Mellows's writings clearly shows, he could scarcely have been more Catholic in his sensibilities. Letters that Mellows wrote just before his execution conflate the language of political and religious martyrdom. He seems to have scrupulously held back from the chaplains near the end, mindful of the Irish Catholic bishops' pastorals against anti-Treaty violence and 'unauthorised murders'. He resignedly wrote in his last hours that 'those who die for Ireland have no need of prayer', although he may have received absolution from a priest at the end.

That same day, in Dáil Éireann, the pro-Treaty Labour Party leader Tom Johnson TD condemned the manner of the four executions. In 1958, however, the then president of the High

Court, Cahir Davitt, who had served as a judge of the revolutionary Dáil courts and was the first judge advocate general of the defence forces of the provisional government in 1922, would write that 'as a drastic means of ending the incipient campaign of assassination of Dáil Deputies', the success of the policy of execution 'was immediate and conclusive' (BMH WS 1,751). Ernest Blythe, the Dáil's Minister for Trade in 1922, later revealed that a day or two after O'Connor and the others died, W.T. Cosgrave – as head of government – had a difficult discussion about the executions with a senior member of the Catholic hierarchy. Cosgrave insisted that the government's 'only false step in the whole business' had been its use of the word 'reprisal' – which was to echo down the years (*Irish Times*, 19 Nov. 1968).

Mellows sent his mother a dignified message, 'It is this: let no thought of revenge or reprisals animate Republicans because of our deaths. We die for the truth.' He wrote that vindication would come, 'brothers in blood will before long be brothers once more in arms against the oppressor of our country – Imperialist England. In this belief I die happy, forgiving all as I hope myself to be forgiven.'

Not everyone was so forgiving. Later that month, Emmet McGarry, the very young son of Seán McGarry TD, died horribly of burns when armed men set fire to his family home in Fairview, Dublin. His sister and mother were seriously injured. McGarry was a pro-Treaty veteran of both the 1916 Rising and the War of Independence. Weeks later, his electrical business was blown up. On 12 January 1923, Senator Oliver St John Gogarty, who had been Arthur Griffith's doctor, was taken by gunmen from his home and threatened. He managed to dive into the ice-cold River Liffey and escape. There were many victims of the Civil War before it ended.

SPRING 1923

A brown Lieutenant and his men,
Half dressed in national uniform,
Stand at my door, and I complain
Of the foul weather, hail and rain,
A pear-tree broken by the storm.

THE BITTER ENDGAME

B y late 1922, the anti-Treaty side had no prospect of winning or of gaining major concessions from the government. Neither side enjoyed a happy Christmas. The exact financial cost of widespread damage to infrastructure throughout Ireland is unknown, but the new state, not a rich one, was burdened by harm already done and by the great expense of reconstruction. Vicious skirmishing was to persist for some months in early 1923, adding to the legacy of bitterness.

Those against the Treaty who had sought the greatest changes were perhaps the greatest losers. Paradoxically, one of the ways in which their republican cause suffered was that Griffith and Collins, the two members of pro-Treaty government most actively ambitious for all-Ireland developments, were dead. The pair had the measure of the British government from their negotiations, and might have faced it down on the border question and the Boundary Commission had they lived. Cautious men now controlled the Irish government, and the influence of a socially conservative Catholic Church was strengthened.

De Valera would soon extract himself from the Civil War by quitting Sinn Féin with his supporters and by entering Dáil Éireann as a new party, Fianna Fáil.

Throughout Ireland people looked forward to 1923, hoping

that Spring would bring an end to violence. Editors and others called for peace. The editor of the *Connacht Tribune*, for example, wrote on 23 December 1922 that 'Christmas inevitably brings up visions of happy firesides, of the full glory of the family life, which is the strength of every people, maintained inviolate and inviolable.' But he also noted that 'winter blasts may rage bitter and cruel outside', and that 'Christmas 1922 falls upon an Ireland riven with the saddest of all strife – the strife of brothers – whose economic life is ebbing, where joy has been turned to sorrow, where bread and work are for many but cannot be because of the conditions that we ourselves have brought about.' That same week, in the *Freeman's Journal*, Una McClintock Dix, an enthusiast for the Irish language and the wife of a renowned bibliophile, suggested a truce: 'Let us put away pride and bitterness, and remember we are Christians and brothers. Each side has much to forgive [....] To both sides I would say, "You are ruining your ideal (of democratic government on one side, and of complete independence on the other) by the violent methods you use." Nothing founded on force lasts.'

The new year 1923 did not immediately see each side put away their arms, and Spring was about to bring some final acts of viciousness and a further waste of lives before open hostilities came to an end.

BALLYSEEDY SLAUGHTER

As the war dragged on through winter into 1923, the anti-Treaty IRA continued to kill soldiers of the National Army and others who upheld the new, democratic state. Some unlawful killings by pro-Treaty forces added to the reservoir of bitterness. Dublin, for example, had a 'murder gang' that unlawfully executed prime anti-Treaty IRA suspects in the capital.

One of the most notorious incidents outside Dublin occurred at Ballyseedy, Co. Kerry on 7 March 1923. The *Cork Examiner* reported:

> Nine irregular prisoners were killed and three National Army officers wounded in a mine explosion at Ballyseedy, near Tralee, on Wednesday morning. Four irregular prisoners were killed and two of the troops wounded in a similar manner at Muckross, near Killarney. The entire thirteen prisoners were mangled almost beyond recognition; portions of their limbs and flesh, with pieces of their clothing, were found adhering to trees and strewn along the road and fields over a hundred yards from the scenes of the explosions. Following the killing of six troops by a trap mine at Knocknagoshel the previous morning, the awful tragedy created consternation amongst the people.

The account of the dreadful occurrences given at the G.H.Q. Tralee [the National Army's local headquarters] is that a series of mine traps were laid for the troops. A party of troops proceeding from Tralee to Killorglin encountered a barricade of stones on the road at Ballyseedy, and in view of the Knocknagoshel fatality, did not attempt to remove the obstruction, but returned to Tralee and brought out a batch of prisoners, who were instructed to remove the barricade. Whilst engaged in doing so a trigger mine exploded, killing nine prisoners.

Stephen Fuller, one of those believed dead at Ballyseedy, was somehow blown clear and survived, unknown to the National Army. His version of events contradicted the official account that the mine being cleared was detonated accidentally. Fuller later became a Fianna Fáil TD.

On 12 March at Bahaghs, near Cahersiveen, Co. Kerry, another five prisoners were killed in similar circumstances. It was soon being claimed in respect to these incidents in the county that mines planted by the anti-Treaty IRA had been detonated deliberately by the National Army to kill anti-Treaty prisoners, who were allegedly beaten, tied up or even shot first. Questioned in Dáil Éireann about the matter on 17 April 1923, General Richard Mulcahy pointed out that the National Army had already suffered sixty-nine men killed and 157 wounded in Kerry – 'seventeen lost their lives guarding food convoys to feed the people in outlying districts.' He told the Dáil that the work of removing 'a large number of road barricades' that remained in Kerry would continue to be done by anti-Treaty prisoners. He added, however, that in all cases of such removals, steps should be taken 'by the use of some grappling implements or the discharge of newly-placed explosives to disturb the obstruction with a view to detecting any trap mines before removal by the prisoners of the material from the road'. The National Army commander in Kerry, Paddy O'Daly, is allegedly countenanced these deadly reprisals and other outrages. He was also accused of attacking on two women in Kenmare, in 1923, but escaped prosecution for it.

Decades later it emerged that, after the Civil War, senior Gardaí in 1923 sent the government an account of events at Bahaghs that flatly contradicted the official version. They stated that the prisoners had been shot before their bodies were thrown on a mine and blown up, and that some local reprisals were organised by certain National Army servicemen nicknamed 'the visiting committee' (*Irish Times*, 31 Dec. 2008). In 1924, Dorothy Macardle published her sixty-page *Tragedies of Kerry, 1922–23*, commemorating Ballyseedy. It was to run to at least nine editions. In 1959, a large and graphic memorial was unveiled at Ballyseedy, its sculptor Yann Goulet being a Breton nationalist and alleged Nazi collaborator who had left France for Ireland, where he sculpted several IRA memorials (*The Guardian*, 6 Sept. 1999). Into the twenty-first century, the Ballyseedy unlawful killings have been used to boost 'militant republicanism'.

Whatever about *unlawful* reprisals in the field, the public generally seems to have tolerated lawful military trials and official executions by the state. In *Defending Ireland: The Irish State and Its Enemies Since 1922*, Eunan O'Halpin pointed out in 1999 that the use of draconian laws did not provoke a crisis of legitimacy for the Cosgrave government, 'on the contrary, the evidence suggests that the majority of the people accepted these laws as necessary for the suppression of disorder [...] the savagery of the laws and the way in which they were applied were vitiated by the lawless ambiance and undisciplined ruthlessness of the IRA's own campaign.' Seán Enright's *The Irish Civil War: Law, Execution and Atrocity* (Dublin, 2022 edition) is a useful source for details of local violence.

In the twenty-first century, Stephen Fuller's son Paudie – himself a sometime Fianna Fáil councillor – has disclosed his father's reluctance ever to talk about the Ballyseedy incident in detail, even as they worked on their farm together (*Irish Times*, 10 March 2003 and 11 Dec. 2015), 'He held no bitterness against those who tried to blow him up; in fact he was full of forgiveness. My father once said to me that the Civil War divisions should not be passed on to the next generation.'

Old Comrade: A badge honouring the anti-Treaty IRA Chief of Staff Liam Lynch after his death in 1923. Courtesy National Library of Ireland [MS 13,712/2/19].

Liam Lynch Killed

On 10 April 1923, while fleeing the National Army at the foot of the Knockmealdown Mountains in Co. Tipperary, the anti-Treaty IRA chief of staff Liam Lynch was shot and seriously wounded. Some of his companions tried to carry him away but abandoned their efforts as National Army troops drew near. He was taken to hospital in Clonmel, where he died on the following day.

During the War of Independence, Lynch had shot a British officer and led a raid on the barracks at Mallow, where a large quantity of arms and ammunition was captured. British troops subsequently sacked Mallow, and it is said that they killed two other men named Lynch during their search for the IRA commandant.

At the outset of the split that followed Dáil Éireann's approval of the Treaty, Lynch worked with Michael Collins to effect some kind of reconciliation, and also to plot a militant strategy for armed action in Northern Ireland. Both men were on the supreme council of the shadowy Irish Republican Brotherhood. They entertained the unrealistic idea that the new Irish Free State might somehow adopt a republican constitution while simultaneously complying with the terms of the Treaty agreement with Britain. The IRA activists who seized the Four Courts did not entirely trust Lynch, thinking him too reluctant to fight the emerging state. Nonetheless, they mended their disagreement with him as the government moved to retake the Four Courts. The National Army arrested Lynch at that time, in June 1922; however, still hopeful that he might soon opt for peace rather than war, the government let him go. He turned out not to be a force for compromise and took charge of the campaign in Munster against the provisional government. 'He has since been much sought for,' reported the *Irish Independent* on 11 April 1923.

Two days later, the same newspaper reported that Lynch lay in state in Clonmel for a day after he was shot and that among those who passed his open coffin in respectful silence then were members of the pro-Treaty National Army and of the Civic Guard, 'most of whom had been comrades of, and fought alongside the deceased in the Anglo-Irish struggle'. Lynch was succeeded as IRA chief of staff by Frank Aiken, a future Fianna Fáil Minister for External Affairs, who is said to have been with him when he was shot.

Meanwhile, at Adrigole, near Glengarriff, Co. Cork, there was a reminder that anyone could pay the price of the continuing civil strife. National Army soldiers had encountered a group of anti-Treaty fighters. There was firing, 'Two irregulars and one girl [Margaret Dunne] were shot dead. Lieutenant Cassidy was wounded' (*Cork Examiner*, 21 and 23 April 1923). Dunne's death certificate reveals that the 'girl' was a single woman, aged 26, who worked as a goods clerk and who died from shock and haemorrhage caused by a bullet wound.

SUSPENSION AND CEASEFIRE

On 27 April 1923, the anti-Treaty IRA chief of staff Frank Aiken ordered his forces to 'arrange the *suspension* of all offensive operations' from midday on 30 April. The combatants were to 'take adequate measures to protect themselves and their munitions'. At the same time, Éamon de Valera announced that his shadow 'Government of the Republic', set up before Christmas, was now 'anxious to contribute its share to the movement for peace'. Most of its members were already in custody.

De Valera was now willing to negotiate an immediate cessation of hostilities on the basis of six democratic principles. These included the principle that the military forces of the nation are the servants of the nation and are amenable to the national assembly when freely elected by the people.

De Valera also pronounced the basic principle of submission to the decision of the people as expressed by a majority vote of the adult population. He could not resist carping, adding that this was 'not because the decision is necessarily right or just or permanent, but because acceptance of this rule makes for peace, order and unity in national action, and is the democratic alternative to arbitrament [deciding of a dispute] by force'. His pro-Treaty opponents surely thought 'it's better late than never'. The *Freeman's Journal* wrote, 'This is specifically the principle upon which Mr de Valera proclaimed war ten months ago, and in resisting which he has been, as far as lay in his power, destroying the country.' It wondered if the announcement was a ruse. However, following some explosions at the weekend, the suspension came into effect. 'Unlike the truce of July 11, 1921 [between Irish and British forces], the suspension of hostilities in Dublin today was not marked by any formality,' reported the *Cork Examiner*.

In his statement, de Valera had also asserted the right to enter parliament without having to face 'any political oath, test or other device'. He did not get his way on this. Only later was the oath abolished.

Before the end of May 1923, the IRA's suspension became a full *ceasefire*. The government had declined de Valera's terms, so Frank Aiken ordered that his people 'dump' (i.e. store) their arms rather than surrender them. The government faced down a hunger strike by anti-Treaty prisoners in 1923, with two men dying during it. Up to twenty thousand anti-Treaty prisoners were being held at the time.

On 3 July 1923, the anti-Treaty Noel Lemass – brother of a future Taoiseach – was abducted and then tortured and killed. His body was found three months later, dumped in the Dublin Mountains. Nobody was ever charged with his murder.

In August 1923, de Valera was arrested at an election rally in Co. Clare and spent eleven months in jail. Within two years of his release, he left Sinn Féin and founded Fianna Fáil. He returned to Dáil Éireann in 1927, deeming the oath now merely 'an empty political formula'. His new party was to offer voters a choice that its critics have claimed proved not very different in practice from that of W.T. Cosgrave's pro-Treaty Cumann na nGaedheal party or its successor Fine Gael.

When the rump of Sinn Féin that remained outside Dáil Éireann after 1927 later sought control of funds that Sinn Féin had collected before 1922, the Irish High Court found that it was not in any legal sense a continuation of the body which existed in 1922 'and which had melted away in the course of that year as a result of the political strife culminating in the Civil War.' In the decision of 1948 (Buckley v. Attorney General (No. 2) (1950), 84 *ILTR*, 9), Mr Justice Kingsmill Moore also remarked that 'Even now Irish politics are largely dominated by the bitterness between the hunters and the hunted of 1922.'

Estimates of casualties in Ireland's Civil War vary, but it seems that at least one thousand five hundred people died, and maybe many more. They remain unlisted. Thousands of others were wounded. Lives were traumatised, property wrecked and the infant state burdened by great damage to its infrastructure. Normal politics were poisoned. The death toll may seem small compared to that of civil wars elsewhere. But the conflict made up in bitterness what it lacked in body count. On his Irish Story website, John Dorney suggests that the absence of agreed figures 'reflects not so much the impossibility of discovering how many died as the lack of will to do so [...] the internecine bloodshed seemed so futile in hindsight. What was the point of dragging up what neighbours and in many cases former comrades had done to each other?' *Spiritual Wounds* (2002), written by Frank Aiken's great-granddaughter Síobhra Aiken, is a vivid account of the personal trauma that the Civil War involved for many. It is a sobering reminder of the harm done.

COMMEMORATION AND CRIMES

Ireland is sprinkled with memorials to people who died in the War of Independence and the Civil War. Seldom do such memorials recall civilian victims.

Monuments, erected with or without official approval, may lend themselves to a lasting interpretation of events that is not only biased but also factually wrong. Common decency and a fear of the consequences of removing them are factors in their remaining as landmarks. An independent inventory of all monuments to the Civil War dead, including their dates of repair, would be revealing. In recent decades, political groupings have constructed many new monuments to rebels of 1798 and 1916–23. This underlines the continuing significance of commemoration, a significance that should be interrogated.

In her work on ethical commemoration, women and the Irish revolution, Linda Connolly questions who has been remembered and how. As an invited participant in the *Machnamh 100* series of seminars organised by President Michael D. Higgins at Áras an Uactaráin, for example, she spoke in May 2021 of some of the victims of sexual crimes during the Irish Civil War. These included Margaret Doherty in Foxford, who was a member of Cumann na mBan assaulted by three National Army soldiers, and Eileen Mary Warburton Biggs, who was a Protestant woman in Dromineer raped by members of the local anti-Treaty IRA – incidents 'documented in great detail in key archives', where 'alleged perpetrators are named and always acquitted'. Elsewhere, in an article in *History Ireland* (Nov./Dec. 2019), Connolly points out that in 2003, the National Graves Association re-erected two monuments to a brother of two of the Dromineer accused, himself the Tipperary IRA commander of their unit and a fugitive suspect following that crime in 1922.

The unqualified commemoration of those associated with, if not convicted of, sexual crimes is rarely if ever confronted and so appears socially unproblematic. More generally, memorials to those involved in the attempted overthrow of the emerging new Irish Free State by assaulting or killing soldiers, or by burning or blowing up the property of non-combatants, are often uncontested. Yet stone speaks to new generations in ways that a text may not. Memorials send a clear signal of what is worth honoring and what may be thought to constitute acceptable political activity in a democracy.

What does the absence of any annual 'independence day' public holiday to mark the foundation of the democratic Irish Free State in 1922 say? The forced compromises of the years 1921 to 1923 constituted a qualified victory, one marred by fratricide. Introducing some Royal Irish Academy commemorative essays, available via RTÉ's Century Ireland webpages, historians Darragh Gannon and Fearghal McGarry suggest that 'Although their role in founding the state, and defending it from republican violence, would become an important part of their political identity, treatyite politicians proved more reticent than their opponents in commemorating the civil war, for whom it provided a rallying cause and a refuge from demoralisation.'

Legacy and Lessons

After its victory in 1923, the pro-Treaty government still faced military strains. As Maryann Gialanella Valiulis has observed, 'a strong possibility existed that, unless the government acted quickly to establish its control, the army could remain the dominant force in Irish politics for years to come' (*Irish Historical Studies*, 1988). The new National Army notably included older pro-Treaty IRA officers, as well as many fresh recruits.

Only following a brief and suppressed mutiny by about fifty army officers in March 1924 did the state settle into a conventional democratic relationship with its army.

The Civil War had caused immense damage to the fabric of the new state. In Dáil Éireann on 19 December 1923, Minister for Agriculture Patrick Hogan TD suggested that the Civil War had cost Ireland £50 million – roughly €3 billion in today's terms. In 1986, in her *Irish Civil War and What It Still Means for the Irish People* (p. 56), Frances M. Blake – who also edited the anti-Treaty Ernie O'Malley's *The Singing Flame* – wrote that even 'a most conservative estimate' of £30 million would have represented 'a disastrous sum by the money values of the time for the already impoverished 26 counties'.

General elections after the Civil War reflected a great divide in Ireland that was to characterise public life throughout the twentieth century. Yet in a way the results were surprising. For in 1923, and in the two general elections of 1927, the pro-Treaty side (by then Cumann na nGaedheal) won 63, 47 and 62 seats respectively (out of 153), but de Valera's anti-Treaty side (which largely became Fianna Fáil in 1927) won 44, 44 and 57 seats. It was clear that neither encouraging civil war nor losing it had rebounded fatally against de Valera politically. In 1932, his Fianna Fáil party formed a government with the support of the Labour Party, de Valera having found a way to overcome the hurdle of a parliamentary oath that had once seemed insurmountable in principle. His party went on to dominate the Irish political landscape throughout the twentieth century.

After de Valera quit Sinn Féin and took many of his followers and TDs into his new Fianna Fáil party, the rump of Sinn Féin (and later 'Provisional Sinn Féin') continued to have an unlawful armed wing that was ostensibly superior to its members in certain decision-making. Some of the unlawful IRA's 'chiefs of staff', including Frank Aiken (1923–5), Seán MacBride (1936–37) and Martin McGuinness (1978–82), later enjoyed mainstream political careers.

On 10 July 1927, Kevin O'Higgins TD, still a minister in government and long associated with tough decisions during the Civil War, was shot dead in Booterstown, Co. Dublin by members of the anti-Treaty IRA ostensibly acting on their own initiative. He had not escaped the bitterness.

In 1981, Danny Morrison, then the publicity officer of Sinn Féin, infamously asked delegates at its annual *ard fheis* in Dublin, 'Who here really believes we can win the war through the ballot box?' In the silence that followed, he added to applause,

'But will anyone here object if, with a ballot paper in this hand, and an Armalite in this hand, we take power in Ireland?' (*Irish Times*, 2 Nov. 1981, page 7).

On 29 May 2022, the *Sunday Business Post* published a RedC opinion poll showing that within the Republic of Ireland, more voters had expressed their first preference support for the Sinn Féin party (36 per cent) than for Fine Gael and Fianna Fáil combined (35 per cent). An *Irish Times*/Ipsos poll of July 2022 confirmed this level of support for Sinn Féin, while giving the other two parties combined 38 per cent. Sinn Féin is already politically dominant in Northern Ireland and may soon come to power in the Republic. Its detractors fear that some form of IRA army council still exerts influence on its decision.

On 21 August 2022, the Taoiseach and leader of Fianna Fáil Micheál Martin and the Tánaiste and leader of Fine Gael Leo Varadkar spoke from the same platform at Béal na Blá, in a ceremony marking the centenary of the killing of Michael Collins there. Martin said, 'The bitterness which grew out of the events of the following year [1922–3] showed how much was lost in this place.' Their appearance together was a welcome gesture of reconciliation by men whose parties are now partners in government for the first time. Given the prospect of the present Sinn Féin being the largest party in Dáil Éireann after the next General Election, they may have had in mind a sentiment said to have encouraged members of the American Continental Congress to sign the Declaration of Independence on 4 July 1776, namely that 'we must hang together, or else we shall assuredly hang separately.' Martin acknowledged the achievements of the Irish state, a state that the founder of his party rejected before becoming a pillar of it. With Martin taking the opportunity also to reproach for cynicism the present Sinn Féin (while not naming it), there was surely an unintended irony in the head of a party founded by Éamon de Valera proclaiming that 'our great revolutionary generation radically changed our possibilities and every major piece of progress our country has secured since then has been through centrist and democratic politics'. It had taken de Valera some time to be converted again to democracy and moderation after first supporting a civil war that failed to achieve its objectives of overturning Dáil Éireann's acceptance of the Treaty and destroying the provisional government of 1922.

Civil War tensions have not gone away. Nor have the tensions inherent in Britain's continuing presence on the island of Ireland gone away. In 1920, the UK parliament deliberately carved Northern Ireland out of the nine counties of old Ulster, in order that the unionists of Northern Ireland's six counties might enjoy a stable two-thirds majority that they would not have had if the whole province of Ulster constituted Northern Ireland. Prior to the UK Government of Ireland Act 1920, Ireland had been a single political unit. Since 1920, demographic changes have significantly altered the balance of power within Northern Ireland. Sinn Féin recently became the largest single party in the local parliament at Stormont. At the same time, the United Kingdom's decision to leave the European Union, against the wishes of the majority of people in both Northern Ireland and Scotland, has rekindled emotions around the question of an Irish border.

After 1921, the expectations of Griffith and Collins relating to the Anglo-Irish Treaty's provision for a boundary commission were disappointed, with the border remaining unchanged. Today, the expectations of the Irish government in respect to British intentions concerning the recent UK–EU 'Brexit' treaty are also proving problematic, raising as they do the spectre of a harder border on the island of Ireland. As part of Brexit, Britain and the EU agreed a special protocol to avoid the Irish land border becoming more obstructive and to protect the benefits of the 1998 Belfast 'Good Friday' Agreement once the United Kingdom left the EU. Yet serious tensions soon emerged concerning the interpretation of that protocol. If Irish people did not learn a lesson from the boundary commission provision of 1921 about relying on the goodwill of a British government, both the Irish and British can still learn from the Civil War about the dangers of indulging national emotions and allowing partisan aspirations to cloud objective judgments.

It is worth recalling the extraordinary, neglected speech by Éamon de Valera to a private session of Dáil Éireann on 22 August 1921, when he wished to get Treaty talks started. He told deputies then that any county in Northern Ireland – which had its own parliament – should be free to vote itself out of an Irish republic and that he was against using violence to force northern counties into a new state. The official Dáil report records him as saying, 'They had not the power, and some of them had not the inclination, to use force with Ulster. He did not think that policy would be successful. They would be making the same mistake with that section as England had made with Ireland.' He added, 'He would not be responsible for such a policy.' De Valera acknowledged that 'Ulster would say she was as devotedly attached to the Empire as they [Dáil deputies] were to their independence and that she would fight for one as much as they would do for the other.' De Valera's speech that day was received with some 'dissatisfaction, apprehension, and confusion' (John Bowman, *De Valera and the Ulster Question 1917–1973*, pp. 54–5). But de Valera had met Prime Minister Lloyd George alone four times in London, in July 1921, and knew what was possible when it came to Ulster. Violent fantasies could not force into existence a thirty-two-county Irish republic.

On 18 June 2022, the editor of the *Irish Times* proclaimed optimistically that the Civil War's legacy 'has all but washed through the political system' today. Nevertheless, having formerly been for some years a council member of the Glencree Centre for Reconciliation, the present author has seen at close quarters how even well-meaning and rational people persistently tend to complete dialogues with 'the other side' by fundamentally restating their basic starting point – even if modified to a certain extent. Reconciliation is a slow process.

What participants on both sides of the Civil War had wanted was a peaceful and prosperous united Irish state, but they differed about how to achieve it. If and when the fateful day comes that a majority of people north of the Irish border vote under the Belfast Agreement to exit the United Kingdom and wish to create a united Irish state, loyalist resistance may again raise the prospect of that outright civil war between Irish unionists and nationalists that was strongly feared in 1922. Within the nationalist camp alone, relations could be severely strained between the present Sinn Féin and the two main political parties that emerged from the original Sinn Féin almost a century ago. Given that the British government may again respond in ways that pertain at least as much to its own domestic priorities as to any other consideration, Irish political parties should proceed with caution and generosity in an attempt to achieve co-operation and unity through peace for future generations.

The Civil War ought to have taught Ireland a very bitter lesson. Yet a residual reluctance in some quarters to condemn anti-Treaty violence has dogged Irish politics. Atrocities on the pro-Treaty side do not excuse ambivalence in respect to the use of force against a democracy.

The Belfast-born painter John Lavery was back in Ireland when Michael Collins died. Lavery immediately obtained permission to paint the corpse which was laid out in the mortuary chapel of St Vincent's Hospital in Dublin, in the late leader's bloodstained uniform. It was an intimate and emotional setting, and this may explain why Lavery most unusually inscribed the canvas in the top corner with the words 'Love of Ireland'. His painting is reproduced on the cover of this book. Perhaps on that terrible day he had in mind a poem written by W.B. Yeats following the rising of Easter 1916, in which Yeats asked in respect to the dead rebels 'Was it needless death after all?' – and 'What if excess of love bewildered them till they died?' An intense feeling of love for Ireland inspired those who risked or gave their lives for independence between 1916 and 1921, and it also motivated many who clashed in the Civil War of 1922 and 1923. But if Yeats in 1916 really believed that it was 'enough to know they dreamed and are dead', this was no longer adequate. Tragic romanticism would not serve well a new democracy in which a substantial majority of the people wished to follow a peaceful path, but where de Valera and others had been prepared to thwart that objective and to seize power by force in order to impose the will of a minority. The intervening facts of the 1918 and 1922 general elections, the establishment of Dáil Éireann and the Dáil's acceptance of the Anglo-Irish Treaty had changed utterly the political landscape. A constitutional, democratic Irish state was born, and democracy must be defended against its enemies.

By the Same Author

Midnight in London: The Anglo-Irish Treaty Crisis, 1921 (2021)

Kenmare: History and Survival – Fr John O'Sullivan and the Famine Poor (2021)

The Enigma of Arthur Griffith: 'Father of Us All' (2020)

An Irish-American Odyssey: The Remarkable Rise of the O'Shaughnessy Brothers (2014)

The Power of Silence: Silent Communication in Daily Life (2011)

Irish Patriot, Publisher and Advertising Agent: Kevin J. Kenny (2011)

Moments That Changed Us: Ireland 1973–2005 (2005)

Fearing Sellafield (2003)

Battle of the Books: Cultural Controversy at a Dublin Library (2002)

The Role of Believing Communities in Building Peace in Ireland (1998)

Molaise: Abbot of Leighlin and Hermit of Holy Island (1998)

Tristram Kennedy and the Revival of Irish Legal Training (1996)

Kilmainham: A Settlement Older than Dublin (1995)

Standing on Bray Head: Hoping it Might Be So (poetry) (1995)

King's Inns and the Kingdom of Ireland, 1541–1800 (1992)